P9-CQK-532

Jean Harding

225-1078

A Sampler of Wayside Herbs

A Sampler of Wayside Herbs

REDISCOVERING OLD USES
FOR FAMILIAR WILD PLANTS

BY

Barbara Pond

ILLUSTRATED BY

Edward and Marcia Norman

GREENWICH HOUSE
NEW YORK

Text copyright © 1974 by Barbara Pond

Illustrations copyright © 1974 by Edward and Marcia Norman

All rights reserved.

This 1982 edition is published by Greenwich House a division of
Arlington House, Inc. distributed by Crown Publishers, Inc. by
arrangement with the Devin Adair Company.

Manufactured in the United States of America

Library of Congress Cataloging in Publication Data
Pond, Barbara.
  A sampler of wayside herbs.

  Reprint. Originally published: 1st ed. Riverside,
Conn.: Chatham Press, c 1974.
  Bibliography: p.
  Includes indexes.
  1. Plants, Useful—United States. 2. Herbs—United States.
3. Plants, Useful—Canada. 4. Herbs—Canada.
I. Norman, Edward. II. Norman, Marcia Gaylord.
III. Title.
QK98.4.U6P66 1982   581.6'1'097   82-9330
                                           AACR2

ISBN: 0-517-385945

h g f e d c b a

DEDICATED TO MY HUSBAND RONALD
for his understanding and encouragement.

Acknowledgments

I WOULD LIKE TO ACKNOWLEDGE my indebtedness and grateful appreciation to: The staffs of the libraries of the Massachusetts Horticultural Society, the Herb Society of America, the Rare Book Room of the Boston Public Library, and the Snow Library in Orleans, Massachusetts; to Mrs. Frank Varga and Mr. Robert Preble who generously lent research materials from their private collections; to Mrs. Charles Shaw for her editorial assistance; and especially to my son George for his help with the text.

—BARBARA POND
August, 1973

And now I shall instance in a few things commonly accounted useless and unprofitable, as in stinking Weeds and poysonous Plants, how that they were not created in vaine, but have their uses. They would not be without their use if they were good for nothing else but to exercise the Industry of Man to weed them out, who had he nothing to struggle with, the fire of his Spirit would be halfe extinguished in the Flesh.

—William Coles
1657

Contents

Color Plates

Introduction

MANY PLANTS NOW CALLED WEEDS were deliberately brought into this country because of their herbal uses. Seeds of others stowed away in holds of ships, hiding in earthen ballast or in fodder and bedding for animals. Colonial housewives brought with them seeds to grow the household medicines, seasonings and cosmetics they needed. They cultivated herbs which were used to keep away moths, scent linens, dye cloth and tan leather. In doing so, they have left a heritage of bright flowers by the wayside and weeds everywhere underfoot. However, not all of the herbs brought here have been abandoned to find their own places in the fields and along our roadsides. Hollyhock, peony, foxglove and others are still cultivated and are now enjoyed for their beauty alone. Often it was the plant that was best able to survive that became despised; invading where it was not wanted, it became a "weed."

But the happy jumble of plants found in vacant lots and bordering roadsides is vanishing all too quickly from our landscape. Blackberries and strawberries once grew in abundance, to the delight of birds as well as passing children, and were recognized by all as worth saving. Until we know infinitely more about the delicate balance of nature, we might reserve judgment before calling any plant a noxious weed, for even the most despised plant may be a delicacy to some helpful insect or food for the larva of an essential pollinator.

The Latin word *arvensis*, meaning "of the field," is part of the scientific name carried by numerous plants and describes their successful invasion into farmland. Recently many have been destroyed by the sprays designed to chemically weed large fields, thus eliminating hand or machine cultivation. Today it is possible, with the aid of weed killers and pre-emergence chemicals, to kill plants without touching them or even seeing them, certainly without understanding their special niches in the living community of plants and animals. The mowing of roadsides radically alters the natural balance and mixture of vegetation, causing perennials, particularly perennial grasses, to increase in proportion to other plants. Annuals, or biennials such as mullein, may not have sufficient time to form seeds before they are cut down. Removing cut weeds from the roadsides and hauling them away as is frequently done robs the soil of nourishment

that would normally be replaced. The run-off of salt sprinkled to melt snow and the exhaust from automobiles take an additional toll.

In a country where the population has moved in such large numbers to the cities, a generation sustained by mass-produced food, patent medicines and synthetic clothing has found little need for herb gardens. Therefore it is exciting to see the re-awakening of interest in herbs particularly among young people who have become more acutely aware of their environment. As they begin to discover the varied uses of familiar plants they may be surprised to find a lifetime avocation. Studying the history of herbs and their uses opens a new window into the past from which one observes not kings, great artists or inventors, but ordinary men and women. They are seen as they go about their everyday lives, trusting in the beneficence of nature, but dreading the witches, demons and elves that were equally real to them. One glimpses a time when there was no manufacturing as we know it today. Medieval housewives and, later, their Colonial counterparts industriously served their families and communities by performing duties we now consider the province of physicians, chemists and pharmacists. They were aided and sometimes misled by information passed down from earliest times. As time passed, information originally gained by trial and error or careful observation was augmented by a large body of folklore and superstition, but a surprising number of ancient remedies and suggestions are still valid. For example, it is somewhat startling to read, as we might in a modern cookbook, John Evelyn's advice written in 1699 that spinach is best when cooked in its own moisture without adding additional water.

One of the earliest and most authoritative herbal texts was written by a Greek physician who served in the Roman army at the time of Nero. Although the Greeks had acquired much of their knowledge of drugs and surgical instruments from the Egyptians, Pedanius Dioscorides wrote *De Materia Medica* at a time when few diseases had been identified. A treatise describing many plants and their uses, it was full of monotonous repetitions. Perhaps its tiresome recitation of similar uses for many herbs reflects the author's desire to list all possible cures for a given illness so that a patient might find at least one medicinal plant that grew in his locality.

Another early physician, Galen or Claudius Galenus, was born about 130 A.D., studied medicine and was appointed physician to the Roman school of gladiators. He developed such exceptional skill in treatment primarily by the use of herbal remedies that he was considered almost an oracle. In another part of the ancient world, Alexandria, a classical school of medicine was founded in the fourth century. It ended, however, in the seventh century with the destruction of that city's great library and the conquest of a large part of the civilized world by the Arabs.

Because of the invasion of Britain in the fifth century by Germanic tribes, Anglo-Saxon was spoken there until the time of the Norman Conquest. Early texts of the period, called "Leech books," were Saxon translations of Latin manuscripts (Old English *læce*, leech, meaning physician). Those which survived the Norman Conquest provide a most revealing glimpse of life during the Dark Ages, containing as they do the superstition and ritual that had crept into the practice of medicine. From the twelfth to the fifteenth century monks carried on the principles of Galen, raising herbs in their monastery gardens to treat the poor and the ill. They copied old manuscripts by hand, relying upon them until the introduction of printing into England in 1426. From then on, many herbals and books on household chemistry and gardening were written and printed; for the first time such knowledge was available to all who could read. Unfortunately, as the English botanist Hulme has commented, "Some old author starts with something that is, after all, only a guess or fallacy, and then generation after generation copy the original statement, some writers being too idle to take any trouble in verifying or disproving it."

The first English herbal was written in 1568 by Dr. William Turner, the father of English botany who was severely criticized for writing in English instead of Latin. In 1597 John Gerard, a London surgeon, published his famous book, *The Herball or Generall Historie of Plantes*. The work was largely taken from one written by the Dutch botanist Rembert Dodoens, but Gerard's own observations of familiar plants gave vitality to it. He was followed by Nicholas Culpeper, who had been apprenticed to an apothecary and later wrote an ambitious text, *Culpeper's Complete Herbal*, which attributed much of the value of herbs to the influence of the planets. His theories connecting astrology and medicine, however, failed to prolong his own life past the age of thirty-eight.

A monumental herbal called *Theatrum Botanicum*, including thirty-eight hundred plants, was published in 1640 by John Parkinson. Then followed the publication of a little gem of an herbal by William Coles, *The Art of Simpling*. Written in 1657, it reveals his childlike appreciation of nature and remains one of the most enjoyable books written in that period. He disputed Culpeper's theories and advanced his idea known as "the Doctrine of Signatures," believing that herbs revealed their uses by their form; going so far as to assume that black walnut husks were good for the scalp, while the convoluted kernels encased in the skull-like shell benefited the brain. One chapter of the book dealt with herbs for animals, making it one of the earliest veterinary texts.

Until the beginning of the eighteenth century, medical knowledge had not advanced appreciably from the time of Dioscorides even though important discoveries had been made in physiology and chemistry. Later, as the professions of pharmacy and medicine developed, use of the old herbals declined. These new sciences, based on information gained in controlled experiments and offering standardized doses of tested remedies, represent immeasurable improvements.

The herbs selected for this book are, with a few exceptions, natives of England or the Continent which were imported to America and later escaped from gardens to grow wild. All of them can be found in the northeastern United States; many are also prevalent in the mid- and far-western states. All the plants have been painted or drawn from living specimens and arranged within the pages that follow according to the blossoming sequence from early spring to late fall. They represent a wide variety of families and have been chosen for their beauty, their colorful histories and, most important, their many practical uses that await rediscovery in our modern world.

A Sampler of Wayside Herbs

LIKE THE FIRST CALL OF THE redwings in the marshes, the first sight of the horsetails, looking like diminutive pinkish asparagus, is a joyful sign of spring. One marvels at the horsetail, one of the few plants (along with algae and fungi) to have survived from earlier ages. Fossil evidence proves its existence three hundred million years ago when this prehistoric plant grew to many times its present size in the carboniferous forests which later formed the earth's coal deposits.

Common horsetail, *Equisetum arvense*, rises from a running rhizome as a short stem tipped with a spore-bearing oval cone. After the spores have dispersed the stem withers away and is replaced by a new green stem with many whorls of jointed, needle-like branches growing from sheathed nodes.

Scouring-rush, *E. hyemale*, rarely branching, usually bears a single slender stem, looking like a jointed green straw. This plant prefers to grow by sandy riverbeds and other moist locations while common horsetail can tolerate drier conditions.

These plants absorb silica which produces a gritty texture in the stems. This abrasive quality is recognized in names such as scouring-rush, gunbright and pewter-wort which reveal their application to cleaning and polishing metal. Cabinetmakers used the plants to smooth their finest pieces and fletchers, the arrow makers, sanded their products to a delicate balance.

Calcium-rich horsetails were once considered beneficial as a hair tonic and as an aid to strengthening fingernails and teeth. People in many countries also found the plant a plentiful source of green and yellow-green dyes.

Today, horsetails remain useful for dyeing, and scouring-rush is used in still another way; segments of the stem are boxed and sold in music stores as abrasives to shape clarinet and oboe reeds. Although not generally considered a delicacy here, the Japanese eat the young spore-bearing shoots before they become gritty.

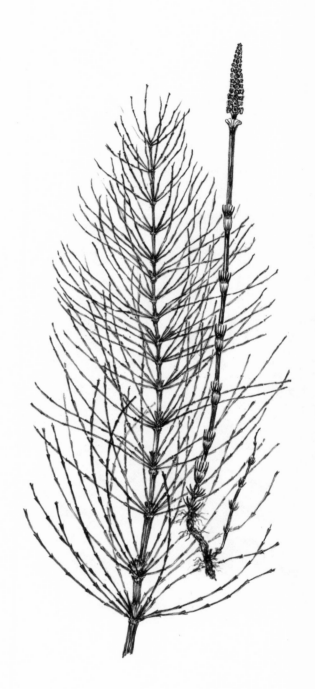

HORSETAIL
Equisetum arvense
Family: Horsetail, Equisetaceae
Fertile stem: Pinkish; sterile stem: green
Fruiting: March—June
Height: Sterile stem up to 2 feet

COLTSFOOT
Tussilago Farfara
Family: Composite, Compositae
Flowers: Yellow
Blossoms: March—June
Height: 3 to 6 inches

COLTSFOOT IS ONE OF THE EARLIEST spring flowers, blooming when yellow crocuses melt away the snow. Many spring flowers are yellow, as if designed by nature to dispel the gray of winter. The dandelion-like blossoms, born on scaly stems, appear first. As the flowering cycle progresses, the leaves finally emerge and at times the leaves and flowers may be found together. The basal leaves, shaped like small hoof prints, give the plant its distinctive name. The tardy appearance of the leaves makes identification confusing and some writers have thought the leaves and flowers belonged to two different plants.

In the past the coltsfoot flower was painted on the doors of French apothecary shops as a symbol of the trade. Coltsfoot was well known as a pectoral herb and was given to people suffering from pleurisy, asthma and coughs. The Greeks and Romans treated asthma by burning this herb on charcoal fires and inhaling the smoke through reeds, alternating puffs with sips of wine. Today there are herbal cigarettes on the market containing blends of coltsfoot, chamomile, rosemary, thyme, lavender and other ingredients.

In earlier days an infusion made from the flower stems was used as a cough syrup. A candy can be made by boiling one cup of coltsfoot tea with two cups of sugar until the syrup forms a hard ball when dropped into cold water. This pleasant confection, with a flavor somewhat like sweet potatoes, makes a soothing cough drop.

THE COMMON BLUE VIOLET AND ITS many hybrid varieties, so abundant in North America, are members of the violet family, Violaceae, which includes all violets, pansies and violas. The English violet, *Viola odorata*, whose name suggests its fragrance, has escaped from gardens and in some areas has become naturalized.

For centuries violets have been used in medicine; the ancients called them cooling herbs. The Greek school of medicine recommended leaf poultices for burning stomachs or inflamed eyes and the Romans made violet wine, reserving some flowers for garlands to ease their headaches. In more recent times the syrup of violets was prescribed for bronchitis and asthma.

It is interesting to note that the blue dye present in many varieties of violets acts like litmus paper; when exposed to acid it becomes red, but alkali turns it yellow.

The fragrance of violet perfume has long been cherished and

rightfully so, for true violet oil is the most costly flower essence. Perfume makers cautiously dilute it with synthetics because the quality of their product is judged by the amount of pure oil in the formula.

Despite their many practical uses, violets were treasured most for sentimental reasons. Blue violets, the symbol of faithfulness, and a single red rose were combined in a bouquet which bashful suitors presented to their ladies to express never-ending love.

Violets were important symbols of love on "Mothering Sunday," an English holiday observed during the otherwise austere Lenten season. On this Sunday servant girls returned to their villages to attend church with their mothers and, for the occasion, brought simnel cakes and violets as traditional homecoming gifts.

THE PANSIES NOW FOUND IN North American gardens are descended from English varieties. One wild species, johnny-jump-up, *Viola tricolor*, so often escapes within gardens and thence from them that it is becoming naturalized here. When planted in borders johnny-jump-up will gaily pirouette throughout the yard, spreading into such unlikely spots as gravel paths and driveways. Even when neglected it seems to thrive almost anywhere with great "joie de vivre."

Shakespeare called it Cupid's flower, and according to Oberon in *Midsummer Night's Dream*, it furnished a powerful love potion:

The juice of it on sleeping eyelids laid,
Will make a man or woman madly dote
Upon the next live creature that it sees.

While the wild pansy's reputation as a love potion may account for its other common name, heart's ease, it was also believed to be good for heart disease.

Both wild and cultivated pansies are suitable additions to an herb garden because their properties are identical. Hybrid pansies, particularly beautiful, need shade and frequent picking if they are to survive summer heat.

COMMON BLUE VIOLET
Viola papilionacae
Family: Violet, Violaceae
Flowers: Deep violet
Blossoms: April–June
Height: 3 to 7 inches
(Plate I)

JOHNNY-JUMP-UP
Viola tricolor
Family: Violet, Violaceae
Flowers: Yellow, white, or purple
Blossoms: May–September
Height: Up to 1 foot

CHARLOCK
Brassica Kaber
Family: Mustard, Cruciferae
Flowers: Yellow
Blossoms: June—August
Height 1 to 2 feet
(Plate II)

CHARACTERISTIC CROSS-SHAPED FLOWERS identify the mustard family; each blossom has six stamens, four long and two short. Although the flowers appear alike, there is great dissimilarity in the sizes and forms of the plants of this family, including as it does such diverse members as brussel sprouts and alyssum.

Brassica Kaber, the species illustrated, is better known as charlock. Its pungent seeds may be substituted in cooking for white and black mustard, *B. alba* and *B. nigra*, which are grown commercially and blended with vinegar and other ingredients to produce salad mustard. Birds enjoy eating charlock seeds but people seem to prefer the boiled leaves as "greens." Farmers, however, regard it unfavorably because it quickly spreads, to the detriment of other crops.

Although unwelcome in the fields, its appearance certainly pleases the eye; Tennyson paid tribute to this pervasive herb in his *Idylls of the King*:

> *In either hand he bore*
> *What dazzled all, and shone far off as shines*
> *A field of Charlock in the sudden sun*
> *Between two showers, a cloth of palest gold.*

Strange as it may seem, black mustard was once an ingredient in love potions. Medicinally, however, it was best known for treating pneumonia. A mixture containing flour and ground seed was applied to the chest as a "mustard plaster" which generated an intense heat endurable for only short periods of time. This stimulating effect of the heat may have inspired a recommendation by Dioscorides: "It is annointed on the lethargical, ye head being first shorne."

CYPRESS SPURGE
Euphorbia Cyparissias
Family: Spurge, Euphorbiaceae
Flowers: Yellow when young, red with age
Blossoms: April—August
Height: 8 to 12 inches
(Plate II)

CYPRESS SPURGE IS OFTEN FOUND GROWING around old foundations and along roadsides. Years ago it was planted in cemeteries and, like myrtle, was sometimes called graveyard weed. This spurge forms large patches resembling miniature forests that intrigue children who sometimes mistake the plants for little pine trees and carry them proudly home.

Culpeper called *Euphorbia Cyparissias* "a strong and violent cathartic and emetic now out of use." Both cypress spurge and snow-on-the-mountain, *E. coronaria*, are frequently grown in gardens and can be a potential danger to children if eaten. The juice of *E. coronaria* is so caustic that it has been used to brand cattle.

The poinsettia, so familiar during the Christmas season, and *E. Lathyris* (called mole plant because it is supposed to repel moles) are closely related to cypress spurge.

Common Blue Violet

PLATE I

PLATE II

Charlock

Cypress Spurge

PLATE II

Horseradish

PLATE III

Strawberry

PLATE IV

HORSERADISH WAS ONCE AN IMPORTANT medicinal herb. An infusion of the root mixed with cold milk was used as a preparation to clear skin blemishes. The raw root was taken internally as a vermifuge and for the treatment of dropsy, or applied externally as a poultice for aching joints and wounds.

Today horseradish has gained new popularity as a farmer's friend by discouraging potato beetles when planted near potato vines. According to Gerard, it also repelled some other plants as well as insects: "Divers thinks that this Horse Radish is an enemie to Vines, and that hatred between them is so great, that if the roots heerof be planted neere to the vine, it bendeth backward from it as not willing to have fellowship with it."

The freshly dug root of horseradish is odorless but shredding releases two substances from different cells which combine to develop the characteristic pungency. Today it is grown commercially for the familiar condiment made by mixing the ground root with vinegar or, as some prefer, with lemon juice. It is served as a sauce with rich meats or oily fish not only because of its piquant flavor but as an aid to digestion. The young leaves of this plant of many uses are an edible potherb and are at their best when combined with milder greens.

Horseradish plants can be easily propagated by root cuttings. An old plant left in the ground and accidentally roto-tilled may produce a number of new plants the following summer. Once established, they are difficult to eradicate because every bit of root must be dug out.

HORSERADISH
Armoracia lapathifolia
Family: Mustard, Cruciferae
Flowers: White
Blossoms: May—July
Height: 18 to 30 inches
(Plate III)

IT HAS BEEN SAID OF STRAWBERRIES that God could have made a better berry, but He never did. Contrary to common belief, the name was not suggested by the practice of mulching the plants with straw, but was derived from the Anglo-Saxon word "streowberrie" describing their growth habit as "strewn over the ground."

Culpeper wrote that strawberries refreshed and comforted fainting spirits and quenched thirst, but he and other early writers were even more concerned with their healing properties. A tea made from the leaves was a tonic as well as a treatment for gout and fevers. The leaves and roots were boiled to make soothing gargles for sore mouths and diseased gums.

The fresh berries have long been known to be a reliable beauty preparation. In times past, sunburned damsels bathed their faces at bedtime with strawberry juice and in the morning restored a ladylike pallor to their skins by washing with chervil water made from that well-known seasoning herb. Cosmetic strawberry preparations are in vogue again; strawberry facial creams, skin lotions and soaps are advertised as modern beautifiers.

STRAWBERRY
Fragaria virginiana
Family: Rose, Rosaceae
Flowers: White
Blossoms: April—July
Height: 3 to 6 inches
(Plate IV)

B LACK WILLOW GROWS ABUNDANTLY ALONG river banks and is both a convenience and a bother to young fishermen. Armed with hooks, lines and bobbers, boys and girls can complete their fishing gear with willow poles but, sadly, can also be sure of a large catch of twigs from the dense thickets and overhanging branches. Willows were much sought by basket makers because the wood was pliable enough to shape. Basket willow, *Salix viminalis*, so named because it ideally suited the craft, was grown expressly for this purpose.

Pussy willows are commonly used for spring bouquets. The large silver-gray catkins of the species *S. discolor* and *S. Caprea* make them especially attractive. If pussy willow branches are to be preserved, they must be cut when the catkins are half open. They should be kept dry as they will continue to grow and leaf out when in water, even rooting easily.

In England willows were called "palms" and were carried in religious processions as well as utilized for church decorations. The Russians called the week before Palm Sunday "Willow Week," a time for gathering the branches for similar use.

In folk medicine willows were a source of salicylic acid, a substance now chemically produced and used as the main ingredient in aspirin. Rheumatism and fevers were common ills in earlier times and were treated with willow bark preparations much as they would be treated by aspirin today.

An important modern horticultural application for a newly found root-promoting substance present in *S. alba* has been suggested by experiments conducted by Makoto Kawase of the Ohio Agricultural Research and Development Center in Wooster. Once the substance has been identified and synthesized, it may be possible to increase the success of herbaceous and woody cuttings by as much as nine times.

PUSSY WILLOW
Salix discolor
Family: Willow, Salicaceae
Catkins: Silver gray
Blossoms: March—May
Height: Shrub to tree

T HE NAME "DANDELION" IS PROBABLY a corruption of the *dent-de-lion* or "lion's tooth," and most likely refers to the shape of the leaf which, according to Mrs. Grieve, resembles a lion's "canine tooth." We now class the dandelion as a weed, but it was once deliberately introduced into the Midwest to provide food for bees. In early spring when bees have depleted their winter supply of honey, the abundant pollen and nectar are welcome fare.

Like snow, dandelions enchant children but dismay adults. The plants are greedy feeders and rob soil of fertility; consequently, gardeners zealously remove them from turf and around plantings. By digging and composting them, however, the stolen nutrients can be returned to replenish gardens and lawns.

If dandelions should regain their former popularity, few of these treasures would be left to idle in the lawn. From early times to the present, all parts of the plant have been useful to man. The flowers once furnished a yellow dye, while the whole herb was used to tint wool magenta. As a folk remedy, dandelions were recognized as beneficial for liver and kidney ailments. The roots were ground, roasted and brewed as a coffee substitute. The tender leaves, available in the spring market, were cooked as "greens" rich in minerals and nutrients. Best of all, dandelion wine was a respectable beverage made and bottled at home by gentlefolk who enjoyed it as a tonic. Today dandelion wine is still made and relished.

DANDELION
Taraxacum officinale
Family: Composite, Compositae
Flowers: Golden yellow
Blossoms: June—August
Height: 3 to 14 inches

DANDELION WINE

4 quarts dandelion blossoms
  (no stems, which are bitter)
1 gallon boiling water
2 lemons, thinly sliced
2 oranges, thinly sliced

3 pounds white sugar
½ pound raisins
1 package yeast
1 teaspoon sugar
1 cup warm water

Cover the blossoms with boiling water; let stand 24 hours, squeeze and strain. Simmer the liquid with the lemons, oranges and sugar for 20 minutes, then set aside to cool. Dissolve yeast with a teaspoon of sugar in warm water. Add this and the raisins to the liquid. Pour into a gallon jug capped with a balloon or a crock covered with cheesecloth. Allow to ferment 14 days, skim, strain and re-bottle.

CHICKWEED HAS SUCCEEDED IN OUTWITTING gardeners by continuing to produce new plants and seeds in late summer and autumn after cultivation has stopped. Some plants may live over the winter, even growing during thaws if they are close to the protection of buildings and can bask in reflected sun. The first spring rains herald the rolling out of a chickweed carpet even before the earth has dried out enough to be worked. The procession of many generations of plants thus starts its march through the year.

But the persistent weed is not without its history of usefulness. Once it was accepted as a cooling herb, a treatment for internal and external inflammation. Because of its nutrients, it was given to build up patients wasted by sickness; yet, conversely, chickweed teas were reputed to slim the obese.

This green herb is good in salads and even better cooked, like spinach, with very little water and served with a pat of butter. At one time chickweed was sold in markets as a potherb. It has also been called "the hen's inheritance" and anyone who has kept chickens will understand why; the succulent greens are their favorite food.

CHICKWEED
Stellaria media
Family: Pink, Caryophyllaceae
Flowers: White
Blossoms: February—December
Height: 2 to 4 inches

SHEEP SORREL
Rumex Acetosella
Family: Buckwheat, Polygonaceae
Flowers: Red to yellow
Blossoms: May—September
Height: 6 to 12 inches

SORREL'S MILD, VINEGARY TASTE ADDS ZEST to salads and soups. Children who have never been served this vegetable may discover it on their own because the tart flavor makes it pleasant for nibbling. This sharpness in the "sour grass" is caused by oxalic acid which is poisonous in large amounts. Dangerous concentrations of it are found in the leaves of garden rhubarb, also a member of the buckwheat family, as are sorrel and dock.

Sheep sorrel grows almost anywhere in the world's temperate zones. The cultivated French sorrel is a delicious vegetable deserving space in more gardens because it is easily grown and, being perennial, furnishes an almost constant supply of greens. During the Middle Ages the vitamin C-rich sorrel was used to prevent scurvy and was also credited as being a cooling herb, a thirst-quencher and a benefit for inflammation and fevers.

Either garden or sheep sorrel may be used in the following interesting recipe taken from *Mrs. Mason's Cookery: The Ladies' Assistant*, by Mrs. Charlotte Mason, published in London in 1793:

SOUP WITH SORREL AND EGGS: Take a knuckle of veal, and the chump end of a mutton loin with a bunch of sweet herbs, pepper, salt, cloves, and mace; stew it very slowly till it is rich and strong; strain it off, and put into it a young fowl, cover it, and let it stew again very slowly; then take two or three handfuls of sorrel, well washed, cut it in pieces not too small; fry it in butter and put it into the soup; let it all boil until the fowl is thoroughly done, scum it very clean, and send it to table; lay some poached eggs round. It may be eaten without the eggs and sorrel, and is very good.

DIFFERING PRINCIPALLY IN SIZE, *Vinca minor* and *V. major* were introduced from Europe and spread from cultivation to woodland borders and roadsides. Ancient Greek and medieval herbalists used both periwinkles for tonic and astringent medicine. During the Middle Ages people sought periwinkle more for the spirit than the body, believing that a bit of the herb worn against the skin was a shield against the Devil's power. Superstition dictated that it be placed over doorways to keep out witches and predictably it served as a charm against snakes, a guise of the tempter since the Garden of Eden.

Vinca had a reputation of insuring happy marriages and uniting in love, faithfulness and affection the man and wife who ate the leaves. If this fails to preserve the love and serenity of matrimony, husbands should remember Culpeper's advice that this herb is a good medicine for females which "may be used to advantage in hysteric and other fits."

A related species *V. rosea*, is a small tropical shrub often listed in nursery catalogs as an ornamental pot plant. It has recently played an important role in cancer research.

Periwinkle, often called myrtle, is an almost ideal ground cover, growing heartily in shaded areas but not densely enough to crowd perennial wildflowers or bulbs. It is easily propagated by cutting bunches of stems six or eight inches long and planting these a trowel's length apart. When kept well watered, the cuttings may grow to cover a sizable area in one season.

PERIWINKLE
Vinca minor
Family: Dogbane, Apocynaceae
Flowers: Blue-violet, rarely white
Blossoms: March–June
Height: Trailing herb

BLUE FLAG, BEARDLESS LIKE ALL NATIVE American irises, is found growing along stream beds or in swampy meadows. Formerly, herbalists advocated taking a decoction of dried blue flag root in carefully controlled doses as a cathartic. Recent investigations have shown that this iris possesses poisonous properties which are an irritant if ingested. There is the potential danger that blue flag when not in flower may be mistaken for sweetflag, *Acorus Calamus*, as both have similar leaf structures and the same habitat.

BLUE FLAG
Iris versicolor
Family: Iris, Iridaceae
Flowers: Violet-blue
Blossoms: May—July
Height: 2 to 3 feet
(Plate V)

YELLOW IRIS IS AN OLD WORLD SPECIES cultivated here from early Colonial times and escaped to brighten swamplands and brooksides with its clear yellow blossoms.

The striking beauty of certain flowers inspired legends in early history. In Greek mythology Iris was the rainbow, messenger of the gods, who transported women's souls to the Elysian fields. When Christianity supplanted pagan beliefs, the rainbow-colored irises, particularly the yellow flags, were dedicated to the Virgin Mary. There is a legend of an old knight who, upon becoming a monk, could not remember any prayer in its entirety. He could only repeat "Ave Maria" continually in his devotions. When he died, yellow irises sprang up beside his bier, each blossom containing the words "Ave Maria" in gold as proof of the acceptance of his simple prayer.

The fleur-de-lis has been the heraldic emblem of France for centuries but there is no certainty of its origin. One account tells of the heathen King Clovis who, near defeat in battle, was influenced to pray to the God of his Christian wife, Clothilde. He won a victory and so replaced the three toads on his banner with three irises, the flowers of the Virgin.

Though rich in lore, this plant has had little apparent medicinal value, although it was recommended for treating some illnesses, including snakebite. It is purported to have been useful as an ingredient in the making of ink and dyes.

Other Old World species, *Iris germanica, I. pallida* and *I. florentine*, were brought to America in Colonial times and since then have occasionally escaped from gardens.

I. florentine was cultivated as the source of orris root, which was used as a stimulant in medicinal preparations. Nowadays the dry powder from the rhizomes, whose fragrance rivals the violet, is best known for scenting soaps and cosmetics and is a fixative agent in potpourri and sachet powders.

YELLOW IRIS
Iris Pseudacorus
Family: Iris, Iridaceae
Flowers: Yellow
Blossoms: May—July
Height: 1 to 3 feet
(Plate V)

SCARLET PIMPERNEL
Anagallis arvensis
Family: Primrose, Primulaceae
Flowers: Scarlet
Blossoms: June—August
Height: 4 to 12 inches
(Plate VI)

ONE OF MANY HERBS SUPPOSEDLY GOOD for the bites of venomous beasts, scarlet pimpernel was also used in early times to relieve ringing ears, aching teeth and other maladies. Although a member of the primrose family, scarlet pimpernel resembles chickweed in its growth habits. In rich humus, the plants attain a size suitable for rock gardens. Another name for it, poor-man's-weatherglass, reflects its habit of closing its flowers before a storm. This little flower gained fame in literature when the Baroness Orczy wrote a novel about the daring English spy, Sir Percy Blakeney, known as "The Scarlet Pimpernel," who saved Frenchmen from the guillotine.

PINEAPPLE-WEED
Matricaria matricarioides
Family: Composite, Compositae
Flowers: Greenish yellow
Blossoms: June—October
Height: Up to 1 foot
(Plate VI)

PINEAPPLE-WEED BELONGS TO AN OLD WORLD GENUS, *Matricaria*, known as wild false chamomile or matricary. Some species are grown in gardens; others are naturalized as weeds. Pineapple-weed, shown in the color plate, is identified by its rayless flower head and pungent pineapple fragrance when crushed. If this weed is allowed to grow in one's garden, it may be justified to the neighbors by informing them that it is good for other plants and that it will also be saved to add to a fragrant potpourri.

German or sweet false chamomile, *M. Chamomilla*, is an annual which self-sows readily. It was used cosmetically as a rinse for blond hair and provides a calming beverage when brewed as a tea. Brides formerly walked down aisles strewn with mint, costmary and chamomile, a custom worth reviving.

Roman chamomile, *Anthemis nobilis*, a true chamomile, has long been made into a bitter tea to relieve fevers, indigestion and nervous diseases. This herb, known as the "plant's physician," was credited with restoring health to ailing plants when transplanted nearby. Today chamomile tea applied to seed flats will combat damping-off, a fungus disease of infant plants. In England it was grown as grass for a fragrant lawn. Another species, *A. tinctoria*, produces a yellow dye, but today is most appreciated as a long-flowering marguerite producing golden blossoms even when planted in partial shade and poor soil. Mrs. Grieve mentions stinking or dog chamomile, *A. Cotula*, as a possible flea deterrent but cautions that it may be poisonous and cause blisters.

Blue Flag

Yellow Iris

PLATE V

Pineapple-weed  *Scarlet Pimpernel*

PLATE VI

Celandine

PLATE VII

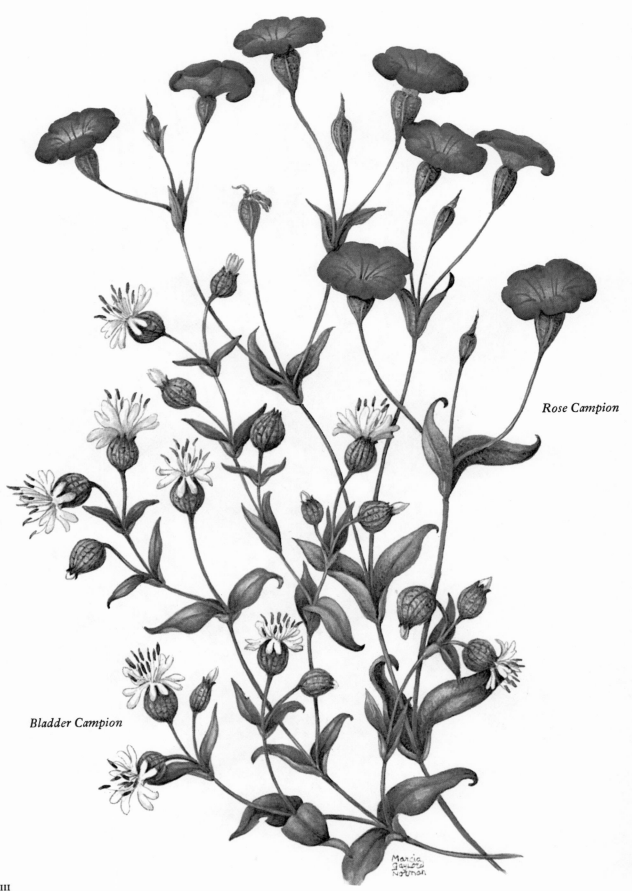

Rose Campion

Bladder Campion

PLATE VIII

CELANDINE, A BIENNIAL OR PERENNIAL MEMBER of the poppy family, flourishes in rich, damp soils. It is a plant of ancient medicinal use and folklore. The name derives from *chelidon*, the Greek word for a swallow, possibly because the plant appeared with the birds' spring arrival and withered at the time of their fall departure. Writings handed down from Greek to Roman scholars and then to early herbalists perpetuated the legend that swallows used this herb to restore the sight of ailing fledglings. Centuries later Gerard discredited the swallow legend but adhered to the early teachings of Dioscorides that celandine was good for sharpening man's eyesight.

Celandine once graced Colonial gardens for both its beauty and its usefulness. In addition to treating the eyes, it was used externally for various skin diseases and the acrid, yellow juice from the stems was applied to remove warts. The plant has been found to be toxic if taken internally, so today its prime value is for the production of yellow dye for wool.

This attractive plant should be welcomed back to shady gardens because it grows easily and blooms over a long period of time. The clear, yellow flowers are followed by long, slim seed pods that have a curious manner of splitting from the base upward to the tip to disperse the seeds.

CELANDINE
Chelidonium majus
Family: Poppy, Papaveraceae
Flowers: Yellow
Blossoms: May—August
Height: 1 to 2 feet
(Plate VII)

ROSE CAMPION
Lychnis Coronaria
Family: Pink, Caryophyllaceae
Flowers: Magenta to crimson
Blossoms: June—August
Height: 1 to 3 feet
(Plate VIII)

BLADDER CAMPION
Silene Cucubalus
Family: Pink, Caryophyllaceae
Flowers: White
Blossoms: June—August
Height: 8 to 18 inches
(Plate VIII)

CAMPION IS THE COMMON NAME for many plants of the genera *Lychnis* and *Silene*. Wise's *Garden Encyclopedia* lists twenty-nine species, a tribute to their ornamental value. Rose campion, or mullein pink, is a markedly handsome member of the pink family with the typical paired leaves. It grows well in sun or partial shade, in heavy clay or sandy loam. An escapee from gardens, it has naturalized in differing areas, springing up in groves where trees have been removed or, surprisingly, on land stripped by bulldozers. These magenta flowers, blazing in a sun-checkered clearing, are reminders that nature knows more about gardening than man can ever learn.

Greek herbalists thought rose campion was an effective treatment for scorpion stings. Some suggested placing campion beside a scorpion to stun it but this procedure seems more precarious than the well-known method of catching a bird by putting salt on its tail. The English often recommended that rose campion be used by the "scorpion smitten," but it is improbable that they had many scorpions to worry about. One suspects that such early manuscripts contain remnants of advice written in warmer climates.

BLADDER CAMPION IS WELL NAMED for its distinctive bubble-like calyxes. In the fall the exquisite urn-shaped seed pods, shown in the black and white illustration, appear to be made of polished wood. They provide interesting material for dried arrangements when combined with bittersweet or other flowers. When locust swarms destroyed the harvest on Minorca nearly three hundred years ago, the inhabitants used this plant as a survival food. And, like the rose campion, it had a reputation for pacifying scorpions.

SWEETFLAG
Acorus Calamus
Family: Arum, Araceae
Flowers: Yellowish green
Blossoms: July—August
Height: 2 to 4 feet

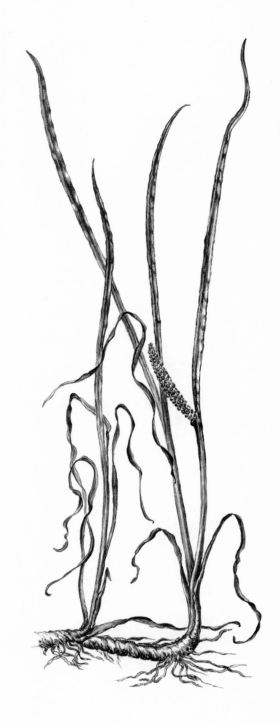

SWEETFLAG OR CALAMUS IS A SEDGE, not an iris like blue flag, although it resembles and grows like our water-loving native irises. Oddly enough, while sweetflag is fertile in America, it is sterile in Europe. It can be identified by its aromatic scent. A plant may smell something like mint, lemon or violet, but whatever the odor, sweetflag has its own long-lasting fragrance and is a valuable ingredient in sachets.

Gerard grew it in his Physic Garden because he considered sweetflag an aromatic tonic good for the digestion. The Old World custom of using calamus for strewing the floors of homes and churches came to the New World with the introduction of the plant. It was scattered about in great quantities and its fragrance must have been delightful.

Sweetflag leaves now are often woven into table mats and baskets. As a flavoring, a bit of the root can be used in place of cinnamon or ginger, and the roots can be candied to make a pleasant confection.

CANDIED SWEETFLAG ROOT: Wash, scrape and cut the roots into sections, then boil them until tender (in several waters if a milder flavor is desired). Prepare a syrup of ½ cup water and 1 cup sugar by boiling until it will thread when dropped from the tip of a spoon. Add the sweetflag root to the syrup and boil for 5 minutes. Drain and roll the sections in granulated sugar.

WILD GERANIUM IS COMMONLY CALLED cranesbill because the seed pod clearly resembles the bird's bill. The family derives its name from the Greek *geranios*, "the crane." Anyone wishing to establish a wild flower garden will find this plant an excellent choice; it readily adapts to cultivation. It might also be planted in an old-fashioned garden as it was in Victorian times when geranium bouquets symbolized "steadfast piety."

Wild geraniums have a thick, perennial root with antiseptic and astringent properties valuable in herbal medicines such as gargles for sore throats. The tanin-rich leaves were bound to cuts and applied to the gums when teeth were pulled. Tea leaves are an equally good tanin source and the styptic effect of both plants is identical. Even today, some dentists encourage their patients to bite down on a tea bag after an extraction.

Herb Robert, *Geranium Robertianum*, is a smaller, more delicate cranesbill geranium with finely cut leaves which once grew in Colonial gardens. It is uncertain which Robert this plant was named for, but it was probably Robert, Duke of Normandy, who commissioned the historic medical text *Ortus Sanitatis*. The leaves of this geranium turn vivid red as they mature, a characteristic which led to the medicinal use of the plant as a treatment for blood disorders, wounds and hemorrhages. This was in keeping with an early theory called the "Doctrine of Signatures" which claimed that diseases were best treated with herbs resembling the affected part of the anatomy.

WILD GERANIUM
Geranium maculatum
Family: Geranium, Geraniaceae
Flowers: Rose-purple
Blossoms: May—June
Height: 1 to 2 feet

BRACKEN FERN
Pteridium aquilinum
Family: Fern, Polypodiaceae
Height: 1½ to 4 feet

Bracken fern, one of the commonest of ferns, is distinguished by the triangular pattern of its bright green leaves. The solitary stems, covered with rust-colored "felt," rise along the length of the creeping rootstock. In its natural environment this fern spreads rapidly, but it is difficult to transplant and its straggly growth habit makes it ill-suited to gardens. It prefers poor, acid soil found in open woods, fields, burned-over areas and along roadsides.

This rather weedy fern, however, does have its virtues; several historic texts report that it sustained the population during food shortages. The roots were ground into flour, then baked into a somewhat unappetizing.but nourishing bread. American Indians peeled the outer fibrous covering off the roots before roasting them.

In early spring the curled young shoots, or fiddleheads, may be boiled until tender. Change the water several times during cooking, then season and serve them with butter as one would asparagus, which they rival. The present-day popularity of fiddlehead greens has made them readily available, frozen and canned, in many stores where gourmet foods are sold.

Always available in season, bracken fern was used in a variety of other ways: it supplied a valuable dye which tinted wool yellow-green and silk gray; the acid in the leaves tanned leather; and a healing ointment was made by boiling the fronds in lard. Woodsmen burned the ferns in campfires to produce a mosquito-repellent smudge, although they did this with caution because they believed the smoke also caused rain.

A legend warns that anyone inclined to gather the spores of this fern on Saint John's Eve will become invisible if he holds them in his hand at the moment of the Saint's birth.

BEARBERRY GROWS AS A DENSE evergreen mat and is easily mistaken for a vine, although it is really a low shrub about three inches tall whose branches may trail two feet from the stem. Carpeting sandy soil with shining green leaves and attractive red berries, it looks like an ideal ground cover. Vacationers persistently attempt to transplant it, usually unsuccessfully because they do not find the main root. This is unfortunate for it is not only disappointing to bring home a plant that dies in a short time, but it is a great loss to the original site where the protective bearberry mat serves to hold the sandy soil.

Some nurserymen take cuttings during late summer or early fall and claim success by rooting them in a sand and perlite mixture and propagating them under carefully controlled conditions. Once established, the plants grow in soil little richer than pure sand.

The berries remain on the plant throughout the winter, providing survival food for wild game and earning other names such as bear's grape, foxberry, crowberry and hog cranberry. The dried leaves are astringent and well known in herbal medicine as a diuretic. They were once used in preparing leather because of a high tanin content. This versatile plant also furnishes either a green or blue-green dye, depending on which mordant (fixative) is added to the dye bath.

ITALIAN WOODBINE/
HONEYSUCKLE
Lonicera Caprifolium
Family: Honeysuckle, Caprifoliaceae
Flowers: Yellow to red
Blossoms: May—July
Height: Climbing vine
(Plate IX)

ALTHOUGH THERE MAY BE THREE HUNDRED species, *Lonicera Caprifolium* and *L. Periclymenum*, the English wild honeysuckles, were among those plants recommended in herbal medicine. The customary methods of infusion and distillation were used to produce rather unreliable remedies for headaches, asthma and dropsy. A tea from the leaves was gargled for sore throats. Gerard found that, "The flowers steeped in oils and set in the sun are good to annoint the body that is benumbed and grown very cold."

However pleasant the fragrance, honeysuckle flowers are not used in making perfume; honeysuckle perfume is usually synthetic or made by combining other floral oils. A native species, *L. sempervirens*, shown at right, is quite unusual because it is scentless.

Gardeners with limited space might follow Parkinson's example when, in 1629, he wrote, "The Honeysuckle that groweth wilde in every hedge, although it be very sweete, yet do I not bring it into my garden but let it rest in his own place, to serve their senses that travel by it, or have no garden."

Honeysuckle will prove itself much too unruly for home grounds unless trellised, but an arch of the vine, with its sweet scented flowers, can make a fitting entrance for an herb garden.

BEARBERRY
Arctostaphylos Uva-ursi
Family: Heath, Ericaceae
Flowers: White, rarely pink
Blossoms: May—June
Height: Trailing 6 to 24 inches

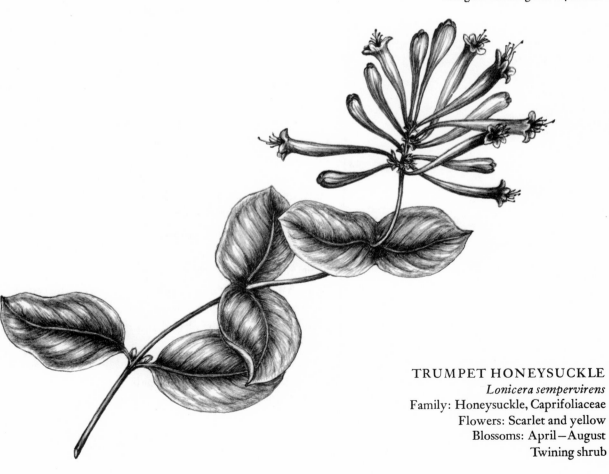

TRUMPET HONEYSUCKLE
Lonicera sempervirens
Family: Honeysuckle, Caprifoliaceae
Flowers: Scarlet and yellow
Blossoms: April—August
Twining shrub

COMMON ST. JOHN'S-WORT

Hypericum perforatum
Family: St. John's-wort, Guttiferae
Flowers: Golden yellow
Blossoms: June—September
Height: 1 to 2 feet
(Plate X)

ALL SUMMER THE GOLDEN-YELLOW BLOSSOMS of the common St. John's-wort brighten the fields and roadsides. As the Latin name indicates, the leaves, speckled with translucent dots, appear to be perforated.

A native of Asia and naturalized from Europe, this much traveled plant is surrounded by folklore and superstition. Some believe that the Druids used the flowers as sun symbols in their religious rites. The blossoms open on approximately the longest day of the year, the summer solstice, which was regarded with awe by early Britons. Christians renamed June twenty-fourth "Saint John's Day" and dedicated the plant to him, but superstitious fears were not easily overcome. On Midsummer's Day witches were said to be most dangerous, and St. John's-wort became a charm hung over doorways to protect against demons and the mischief of such witches and thunderstorms.

Adventure lovers will be pleased to know that anyone who steps on the plant on Saint John's Eve may expect a little excitement. A magical horse will spring up from the ground beneath the person and carry him away; the excursion, however, ends abruptly at sunrise.

St. John's-wort served to cure melancholy, hysteria and madness. An ointment made from its blossoms mixed with melted fat was applied to cuts and bruises. The leaves steeped in water provided both external and internal medication for many ailments.

Today most tree and shrub catalogues list several related plants, some of which are hybrids of English and Japanese varieties. Aaron's beard, *Hypericum calycinum*, makes an evergreen ground cover suited to sunny or slightly shaded locations and sandy soils. When planted eighteen inches apart, they may hide the ground completely within a single season.

Italian Woodbine

PLATE IX

PLATE X

Common St. John's-wort

PLATE X

Wild Indigo

PLATE XI

Common Mallow

PLATE XII

THE BUSHY APPEARANCE, BLUE-GREEN LEAVES and yellow flowers make wild or false indigo distinctive along the roadsides. This native wild indigo belongs to the same family as the true indigo, so well known as a source of blue dye. The term "indigo blue" is a common expression for its characteristic tint.

True indigo was cultivated only in warm climates. India exported it in the form of cubes called "junks," the product of a complicated process which yielded the best blue dye available for woolen yarn. Unfortunately, the blue dye obtained from wild indigo proved to be a poor substitute.

The wild variety was useful in other ways, however. It has been grown by the French perfume industry under the name "genet" for the sweet honey scent of its flowers. Herbalists claimed it was antiseptic, astringent and a febrifuge good for malaria; farmers tied it to horse harnesses and called it "sho-fly-weed," believing that something in the leaves, perhaps an odor, acted as an insect repellent.

Anyone who digs up wild indigo to move it to a garden may be startled the next day to find that it looks coal black. *Baptisia's* curious tendency to turn black when wilted is a positive identification not shared by similar yellow flowering legumes.

WILD INDIGO
Baptisia tinctoria
Family: Pulse, Leguminosae
Flowers: Golden yellow
Blossoms: June—July
Height: 1 to 2 feet
(Plate XI)

COMMON MALVA, OR CHEESES, has button-sized seed pods which resemble a whole cheese shaped like a wheel. The seed pods are edible, but not particularly palatable, and perhaps are most properly served at dolls' tea parties.

Other species of malva, or mallow, were cultivated by the Egyptians, Greeks and Romans who ate the boiled leaves and found medicinal value in the whole plant. Leaves, flowers and sometimes roots were soothing ingredients in herbal cough and sore-throat remedies, while the leaves made handy poultices for bee stings.

The larger members of the mallow family contain tough fibers that were used to manufacture rope, paper, wallpaper and fabric. According to legend, Mohammed wore a garment made from this material. He was so pleased with it that he rewarded the plant by giving it brilliant flowers, thus changing it into a geranium.

Cotton, hollyhock and okra also belong to the mallow family. The herbal roots of another relative, marshmallow, *Althaea officinalis*, provided the unique consistency of the original marshmallow candy. The familiar confection is now made with corn syrup, cornstarch and gelatine, retaining only the plant's name.

The wild musk mallow, *Malva moschata*, is ornamental and transplants well. It, as well as a number of other mallows hybridized by seed companies, are attractive additions to a garden.

COMMON MALLOW
Malva neglecta
Family: Mallow, Malvaceae
Flowers: Pale lilac or white
Blossoms: April—October
4 to 18 inches long, creeping
(Plate XII)

THIS CREEPING HERB HAS SEVERAL colloquial names: teaberry, checkerberry, mountain-tea, and the best known of all, wintergreen. Wintergreen makes an exceptional ground cover over sandy soil, but also needs the shade and humus supplied by the evergreens growing in that environment. The crisp, shining oval leaves interspersed with delicate bell-shaped flowers or bright red edible berries form large contrasting patches on a pine-needle floor. Deer and other woodland wildlife graze on the plants.

Near the turn of the last century, wintergreen was much in demand, and more than a ton of the herb was picked annually. The leaves were fermented to bring out the flavor and then distilled into Oil of Gaultheria. This was recommended for sciatica and rheumatism, even as the Indians had used it in earlier times for the same purpose. Because the oil was known to be a stomach irritant, internal doses were given in gelatin capsules. The green leaves were also used to brew an aromatic tea.

The modern synthetic oil flavors candy, gum and toothpaste, while its fragrance in soaps and shaving lotions suggests fresh-mown hay. The plant is suitable material for terrariums.

BROOM'S MEDIEVAL NAME, *Planta genista*, became the title of an English royal family, Plantagenet. Lankester wrote, "There is strong evidence to prove that Falke, Earl of Anjou, grandfather of Henry II, assumed the *planta genista* as an emblem of humility on leaving for the Holy Land."

She further connects the plant to heraldry by reporting: "From very early times the Broom was a favorite emblem in France. In the year 1234, 'Saint Louis', as Louis IX of France was called, celebrated the coronation of his queen by establishing a new order of knighthood, the Soldiers of the Broom. In 1389, England's Charles VI gave the same decoration to his kinsmen, making them 'Knights of the Star of the Broom-pods.'"

An earlier name, "Sarothamus," came from the Greek words meaning "to sweep" and "a shrub." Culpeper wrote that broom's household use, sweeping, was so familiar that it would be unnecessary to describe it. The tough stem fibers furnished raw material for both paper and cloth. Broom tips, in a potion sometimes containing dandelion root, became a popular medicine for dropsy, an ailment associated with heart and liver conditions.

Today many varieties of broom are sold by nurserymen. They are particularly useful when planted where most other shrubs would struggle to survive because they withstand wind, poor soil and drought.

TEABERRY/CHECKERBERRY
Gaultheria procumbens
Family: Heath, Ericaceae
Flowers: White; berries: red
Blossoms: July—August
Height: 2 to 5 inches

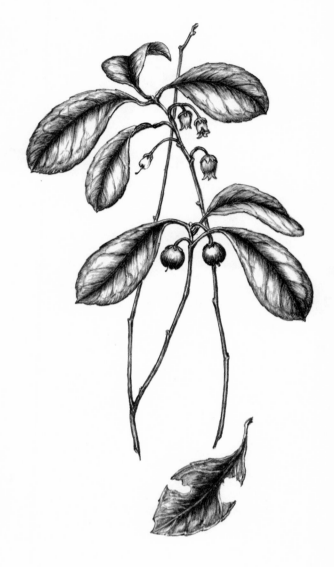

BROOM
Cytisus scoparius
Family: Pulse, Leguminosae
Flowers: Yellow
Blossoms: May—June
Height: Shrub to 6 feet

HEAL-ALL EASILY FOOLS AMATEUR GARDENERS. One or two plants are apt to appear masquerading as flowers. The seedlings so resemble four-o'clocks or other self-sown annuals, that they are carefully passed by the gardener's hoe. They grow quickly, deceiving him with imposing foliage so that he never suspects them to be the scruffy weed of vacant lots. But he would be wise to take solace in the intriguing blossoming spike or head. Individual flowers, similar to mint, are crowded in the rounded bracts, giving the plant a healthy, robust chin-up air.

Heal-all was known in German folk medicine as brunella, a name almost certainly derived from *braune,* meaning sore throat, which was treated with the herb infused and mixed with honey to make a soothing syrup. Many doubt that heal-all lives up to its name, but an old manuscript cites its value as a wound herb and advises combining the leaves with those of bugleweed to make an ointment with a lard base. This preparation was to be stored for use when needed. The text assures that, "Such as are so kind as to keep and administer such helps to the poor, cannot keep a better salve."

THE AMERICAN INDIANS CALLED this herb "white man's foot," because wherever Englishmen colonized, the plantain surely followed. The broad flat leaves, growing close to the ground, inspired plantain's Latin name, *Plantago,* the word "planta" meaning sole of the foot.

Plantain's flower stalks are at least as well known as its leaves. Exceptionally tough and resilient, they resist mowing, and the stems often remain standing three to five inches above a recently cut lawn. This resiliency was depicted by an English author, Edward Hulme, who described the plant's distressing ability to dull the scythe.

Early records credit plantain with positive value as a vulnery, or a dressing for wounds, for both man and his domestic animals. Greek and Roman physicians applied it to wounds, bruises, stings and inflammations. Pliny so thoroughly believed in the herb's healing qualities that he claimed chunks of meat would become "sodden together" if plantain was thrown into the cooking pot.

The very young leaves are edible and might serve as an emergency food if hunger were strong enough to overshadow the tedium of collecting enough for a meal; flocks of sparrows will banquet on the ripening seeds. The seeds have also been gathered along with those of chickweed and groundsel, and the blend was packaged by English shopkeepers and street vendors to be sold as food for caged birds.

SELFHEAL/HEAL-ALL
Prunella vulgaris
Family: Mint, Labiatae
Flowers: Purple
Blossoms: June—September
Height: 6 to 12 inches

PLANTAIN
Plantago major
Family: Plantain, Plantaginaceae
Flowers: White
Blossoms: May—September
Height: 6 to 18 inches

Ox-eye daisy, an Old World plant, escaped from early Colonial gardens and has spread rapidly through our northern states, much to the dismay of farmers. It thrives in pastures, where it grows unmolested by grazing cattle who seem to prefer other forage. Drifts of the white blossoms among the pasture grasses are a most memorable sight, a reminder of the daisy-chains once used at school commencements. The flowers were a young girl's oracle of love, revealing the fateful answer as she repeated for each petal: "He loves me, he loves me not."

Wild English daisy, *Bellis perennis*, opens at dawn and closes at dusk, a distinction which gave the plant its original name, "day's eye." *B. perennis* is a harbinger of the English spring and, in America, garden centers blossom with little baskets of pansies and English daisies before Mother's Day.

Both daisies shared some medicinal properties, beneficial for the treatment of pains, wounds and fevers. In addition, the ox-eye daisy, being a close relative of chamomile, was brewed to make a calming tea. John Evelyn wrote that, "the young roots are frequently eaten by Spaniards and Italians, all the spring until June." But daisies may seem less palatable to anyone who has read that the leaves repel fleas.

OX-EYE DAISY
Chrysanthemum Leucanthemum
Family: Composite, Compositae
Flowers: White, yellow center
Blossoms: June—September
Height: 15 to 25 inches

YELLOW BEDSTRAW
Galium verum
Family: Madder, Rubiaceae
Flowers: Yellow
Blossoms: May—September
Height: 8 to 30 inches
(Plate XIII)

Yellow bedstraw once had varied and important household uses. It was sometimes called "cheese rennet" because it had the property of curdling milk, a necessary step in cheese making. *Galium* comes from the Greek word *gala*, meaning "milk." The yellow flowers colored both cheese and cloth; in Tudor England girls used it for dyeing their hair blond. The roots yield a red dye, not unlike madder, which is a close relative in the plant kingdom.

Because of the old belief that the appearance of plants somehow indicates their medicinal uses, the red extract from the roots suggested to herbalists that bedstraw could be used to stop bleeding. It was therefore prescribed for nosebleeds as well as for hysteria. In 1657, during a time when people traveled on foot, William Coles said herbalists agreed, "the Decoction of Herbe and Flowers being yet warme, is of admirable use to bath the Feet of Travellers, and others who are surbated by long Journeys in hot weather, and for Lackies and such like, where running long couseth not only weariness but stiffnesse in the Sinews and Joynts, to both which this herb is so friendly, that it maketh them to become as lissome, as if they had never been abroad." One might remark that bedstraw was good for both extremities of the body.

Airy mounds of bedstraw growing wild or in a garden invite one to stop and rest. It is not surprising that before the manufacture of springs and mattresses, these plants were used for bedding. Christian legend calls this plant "Our Lady's bedstraw," a manger herb. With its fine whorled leaves and shining yellow flowers, what a lovely bed it may have made for a baby.

JEWELWEED
Impatiens capensis
Family: Touch-me-not, Balsaminaceae
Flowers: Orange yellow
Blossoms: June—September
Height: 2 to 5 feet
(Plate XIV)

JEWELWEED KEEPS BAD COMPANY, growing in moist ground with poison ivy and stinging nettle. The crushed leaves and stems of touch-me-not, however, are a convenient and effective first-aid treatment for the discomfort caused by an imprudent encounter with its neighbors. Euell Gibbons suggests boiling a quantity of the stems and leaves, straining the resulting liquid and applying it after exposure to poison ivy. Since the liquid does not keep well, he recommends freezing some of it to insure a supply when needed.

Anyone who has ever seen this succulent herb after a shower, with the sun sparkling on the iridescent droplets of water still clinging to the margins of the leaves, will appreciate its name. The yellow-orange flower pouches sway on long stems as brilliant ornaments designed to lure hummingbirds to the nectar. In areas where there are no hummingbirds, the jewelweed may also produce cleistogamous flowers. These are quite different self-fertilizing blossoms that set seed without opening.

The name "touch-me-not" may seem illogical to one who has never handled the ripe seed pods, but it is apparent to anyone who has observed that the slightest touch causes a sudden, violent splitting of the linear seed pods into coiling valves which forcibly eject the seeds.

A closely related garden plant, balsam, *Impatiens Balsamina*, has large fuzzy seed pods which stay intact when picked. A favorite children's prank is to say, "this is a caterpillar," while squeezing it into a friend's palm. The floral caterpillar then writhes with a startling effect. *I. sultana*, or "patient Lucy," an old garden favorite, has become increasingly popular with horticulturists for the variety of color of the blossoms which bloom luxuriously in shaded places.

Several writers have called jewelweed edible if picked when young and only a few inches high, but others list it as a potentially dangerous medicine, diuretic and cathartic. The flowers have been collected to make a yellow dye, although this must have been tedious work because of their small size.

Yellow Bedstraw

PLATE XIII

Jewelweed

PLATE XIV

Butterfly-weed

Marcia
gaylord
Norman

PLATE XV

Motherwort

PLATE XVI

BUTTERFLY-WEED
Asclepias tuberosa
Family: Milkweed, Asclepiadaceae
Flowers: Orange
Blossoms: June—September
Height: 1 to 2 feet
(Plate XV)

O N CERTAIN BRIGHT DAYS, butterfly-weed's orange blossoms are covered with butterflies. A naturalist reported counting at least ten different species feeding on the nectar. "Butterfly flower" might have been a more appropriate name for this handsome plant whose brilliant blooms foreshadow autumn.

Much of the butterfly-weed's natural habitat has been destroyed by home building and road construction. As early as the 1930's, the herb was reportedly becoming scarce in some areas where it formerly grew in abundance. People unwittingly kill the plant in trying to save it, because they may not be aware of its long tap root which is easily broken. It can be moved only when dormant or very small, unless a great quantity of earth is moved with it.

Butterfly-weed is a milkweed, although it does not have the cloying fragrance or copious milky juice characteristic of other members of the milkweed family. Asclepidaceae, the family name, honors Aesculapius, a Greek physician and folk hero who was later deified. To the Romans he was known as Asclepius, Apollo's son, and the father of two daughters, Panakis and Hygeia, whose names have been transmitted into English as "panacea" and "hygiene."

American Indians were among the first to notice butterfly-weed's medicinal qualities and took an infusion of its roots for respiratory diseases. Since the roots are poisonous, we must assume their medicine men administered carefully controlled doses. Indians cooked and ate other milkweeds, favoring the young shoots, unripened seed pods and buds. They collected the milky juice to treat their horses' sore backs or dried it near fire to make a chewing gum. Herbalists learned that this native American plant was a pectoral herb and called it "pleurisy root." They also prescribed it for rheumatism, fever, spasms and dysentery.

Gardeners who can offer butterfly-weed a sunny, well-drained location may be pleased to know that nurserymen now propagate the plant. The flowers can be cut or left until the seed pods ripen, adding interest to dry arrangements.

MOTHERWORT
Leonurus Cardiaca
Family: Mint, Labiatae
Flowers: Lilac
Blossoms: June—August
Height: 2 to 4 feet
(Plate XVI)

Motherwort, or lion's tail, is an exotic-looking Eurasian herb introduced here in early gardens. It has escaped to barnyards to join its relative, catnip, in sharing the same fertile soil. The name *Leonurus* derives from the Greek for "lion's tail" and the Latin term *Cardiaca*, meaning "for the heart," recalls the herb's tonic reputation.

This tall, dignified herb had other virtues. The tops and leaves were used to treat insomnia and hysteria, afflictions old herbals described as being "peculiar to women." Culpeper stated that, "It is of use for the trembling of the heart" and that, "drunk in wine, it helps women in sore travail." He continued, saying that it made "mothers joyful," perhaps a reasonable conclusion. However, the herb was sometimes also administered in a sugary conserve to mask its bitterness.

This stately plant is now naturalized, growing abundantly as a weed, although it is still cultivated in gardens for its decorative value and use in flower arrangements. When it is cut and combined with other flowers, few would guess its origin.

Cleavers shows such open affection toward man, with its long stems seeming to reach out for every passerby, that it has been called "catch weed," "grip grass," "loveman" and "snatch weed." The Greeks named the plant *philanthropon* in recognition of its fondness for humans. The stems and leaves are covered with prickles like small hooks and rough burr-like seeds, both designed to assist the weak stems in gaining support from neighboring plants.

Some persons say the seeds make an acceptable coffee substitute and claim that the brewed leaves are good for tea. The roots, like those of Our Lady's bedstraw, provide a red dye. Those not prejudiced against weeds will find that cleavers makes a good-looking houseplant, particularly when trailing from a hanging basket.

Its numerous medicinal uses were related mostly to kidney and skin disorders. According to Culpeper, cleavers made a fine spring tonic, a blood purifier for the body which, thus renewed, would be ready for warmer weather.

CLEAVERS
Galium Aparine
Family: Madder, Rubiaceae
Flowers: White
Blossoms: May—June
Height: Weak stems, 2 to 3 feet

MULLEIN
Verbascum Thapsus
Family: Figwort, Scrophulariaceae
Flowers: Yellow
Blossoms: Late June—September
Height: 2 to 6 feet

THE COMMON MULLEIN, OFTEN SCORNED as a weed, is a very handsome plant tolerating sandy, dry conditions and growing best in alkaline soil. The leaves are covered with a woolly mat of white hairs which reflect the sun and retain moisture. Its presence has sometimes helped archaeologists locate Indian shell heaps, as lime from the shells gives the soil an ideal pH factor for the mullein to flourish in abundance.

During the first year, the biennial mullein's felted leaves are arranged in a large rosette. The following season the plant becomes a pillar of soft green foliage, terminating in a long spike of clear yellow buds. These open almost at random to blossom over an extended period, thus ensuring a prolonged display. The maturing spikes, perhaps harboring hidden insects, attract insect eaters such as woodpeckers. Anyone having a large sunny garden could include a few mulleins without worrying that they will become pests. The few plants that do self-seed can be moved to a site where their large size is welcome.

Mullein has an interesting history of practical and cosmetic use, for example, in poultices and infusions, and in oils to treat toothache, earache and coughs. A floral rinse brightened blond hair and soap made from ashes of the herb was thought to restore color to gray hair. Fresh mullein stalks were dipped in melted fat, ignited and carried as flaming tapers in ceremonial processions. In some Indian tribes, the men smoked mullein mixed with tobacco. The women diapered their babies in the largest soft leaves.

Our Saxon ancestors asserted that, "if one beareth with him one twig of the wort, he will not be terrified with anyone, nor will a wild beast hurt him, or any evil coming near. He dreadeth not any robber, but the wort puts them all to flight."

SEVERAL SPECIES OF SOW THISTLE are so common along road-sides and in waste places that the herb is generally rejected as a weed, but closer examination proves this thistle-like plant to be worthy of notice. The leaves of *Sonchus oleraceus* somewhat resemble those of the dandelion, but grow from the flower stem rather than from a basic rosette. The leaves of *S. asper* clasp the stem with a dramatic sweeping curve that is most decorative.

Ancient Romans credited sow thistle with the same strength-giving reputation Americans attribute to spinach. *Oleraceus* means "good for a vegetable" and it is used both as a salad and potherb. The leaves should be boiled, drained, then boiled again to remove any bitter taste. The tender, fresh new shoots are good mixed with other greens.

Herbal doctors collected and distilled the milky juice, which was thought to be diuretic and cathartic. Other diverse applications even included using the ordinary sow thistle as a cosmetic; it served the ladies as a complexion cream to cleanse the skin.

Not to be overlooked is the succor which this plant, also known as "hare's lettuce," provided wildlife. A legend affirms that hares, when pursued by hounds, stopped and ate the leaves to cool their blood; thus refreshed, they were able to escape.

CATNIP, OR CATMINT, IS A TRUE MINT; its square stems and aromatic leaves allow no uncertainty that it belongs to the family of Labiatae. Native to Europe and Asia, it was imported by Americans who knew its value as a medicinal tea taken for colds, nervous headaches and insomnia. As a culinary herb catnip, like spearmint and peppermint, has uses limited only by the cook's imagination.

Catmint is a well deserved name for the fragrance is indeed intoxicating to cats. Gerard observed: "Cats are very much delighted herewith; for the smell of it is so pleasant unto them, that they rub themselves unto it, and wallow and tumble in it, and also feed on the branches and leaves very greedily."

City cats, accustomed to their almost odorless catnip toys, respond in ecstasy when they encounter a growing plant, sometimes demolishing it. Country cats who have a supply of the herb growing nearby will help themselves to a few leaves in passing, but rarely become as silly over it. Dogs sometimes sample the plant if they have seen a cat's enjoyment of it and don't want to miss a good thing.

Several cultivated species, less appealing to felines, are tolerant of most growing conditions. *Nepeta macrantha* is tallest, about two feet, and is excellent for planting in borders. *N. mussini* and *N. nervosa* form mats less than a foot high and are good ground covers. These will bloom over a long period if the flowers are cut before the seeds mature.

SOW THISTLE
Sonchus oleraceus
Family: Composite, Compositae
Flowers: Light yellow
Blossoms: July—October
Height: 2 to 6 feet

CATNIP
Nepeta Cataria
Family: Mint, Labiatae
Flowers: Lilac to white
Blossoms: July—October
Height: 2 to 3 feet

VIPER'S BUGLOSS
Echium vulgare
Family: Borage, Boraginaceae
Flowers: Blue violet
Blossoms: June—July
Height: 1 to 2 feet

VIPER'S BUGLOSS IS A HANDSOME PLANT of the fields and way-sides, attracting attention by its flowers which start as pink buds, turning as they develop into brilliant, clear blue blossoms. Early manuscripts endow bugloss with the ability to drive away sadness and make the heart joyful. There are, in fact, precious few true blue flowers in nature; their appearance in itself should be enough to brighten a gardener's day. As the flower matures, it produces seeds which look like a viper's head, a resemblance which may explain the superstition that it could counteract viper venom.

Some herbalists concluded that since bugloss might combat the highly toxic viper bite, it would cure all snake bites. Dioscorides, crediting man with some degree of foresight, suggested the cure be taken before the bite. In folk medicine, this plant was prescribed imaginatively for every malady from swollen feet to throat irritation. Even the roots were considered useful, yielding a red dye.

Bugloss is closely related to borage, *Borago officinalis,* cherished in the herb garden for its star-like blossoms of a similar beautiful blue. Both are culinary herbs; the cut flowers may be floated in punch bowls to add flavor and double as a decorative accent. Added to wine, it was recommended for cheering one's temper. Young bugloss leaves may be added to salads, but here caution is advised as some people are allergic to the plant, possibly suffering a reaction to the rough, prickly leaves.

SALT SPRAY ROSE
Rosa rugosa
Family: Rose, Rosaceae
Flowers: Purplish rose or white
Blossoms: July to frost
Height: 4 to 6 feet
(Plate XVII)

THIS HARDY ASIAN ROSE is commonly called salt spray because it seems to grow best along exposed shores. Spreading by means of underground stolens, it forms impenetrable thickets which protect dunes from erosion. Its appeal comes more from the tart, nourishing fruit than from its scatter of single flowers. While still blooming, a bush may be ornamented with green, orange and red fruit or "hips," looking much like cherry tomatoes. These may be enjoyed raw, boiled to make a tea or in jelly where the flavor is similar to quince with honey.

Although satisfactory in making sachets, *Rosa rugosa* cannot produce the quantity of petals required by perfumers. Less than a pound of rose oil can be extracted from ten thousand pounds of petals.

Two roses naturalized from Europe, the dog rose, *R. canina*, and sweet briar or eglantine, *R. Eglanteria*, develop similar but smaller fruits. During the Second World War when England was unable to import citrus fruit, these rose hips were carefully factory-processed into syrup, the English having discovered that rose hips contain twenty times more vitamin C than oranges. Because the hips of the salt spray rose are so large, enough fruit to make a batch of jelly can be gathered in a short time.

SPICED ROSE HIP JELLY

1 quart rose hips	1 teaspoon cloves
5 tart, unpeeled apples, sliced and cored	1 lemon
	granulated sugar

Cut the rose hips into small pieces. Put them with the apples, cloves and lemon and cover with water (add water just until it shows above the fruit). Cook until tender; mash well and strain, using a jelly bag. For each cup of the strained liquid, add one cup of granulated sugar. Boil, stirring frequently, until the syrup threads from a spoon or until a jelly thermometer reads 220° F. Pour jelly into clean, hot jars and cover with melted paraffin.

DOG ROSE, *Rosa canina*

SWEET BRIAR, *Rosa Eglanteria*

EVENING-PRIMROSE
Oenothera biennis
Family: Evening-Primrose, Onagraceae
Flowers: Yellow
Blossoms: July—August
Height: 1 to 6 feet
(Plate XVIII)

THIS NATIVE AMERICAN WILDFLOWER was introduced into Europe early in the seventeenth century and, in England, was cultivated as a root vegetable. During an earlier age, Dioscorides believed that a root concoction could tame wild animals or, if applied to a patient externally, could cure "wild ulcers."

The flowers of evening-primrose, sometimes called evening star, open at sunset and partially close soon after sunrise. They will protect a garden from Japanese beetles for these insects congregate on the blossoms, which they find irresistible. They can then be wisked into a container when they become sluggish in the early morning or late afternoon. In the morning one can sometimes find a small sphinx moth resting in a drooping blossom, a pollinator that stayed up late to drink the nectar.

BOUNCING BET
Saponaria officinalis
Family: Pink, Caryophyllaceae
Flowers: Pink
Blossoms: July—September
Height: 1 to 2 feet
(Plate XIX)

BOUNCING BET CAME TO COLONIAL gardens from England and strayed throughout yards and along roadsides. A sturdy, happy plant with an air of practicality, it appears aware of its homely virtues. Soapwort, another colloquial name, perhaps best suggests its usefulness to man, for anyone with bouncing bet in the yard has an almost inexhaustible supply of dish washing liquid. The plant contains the chemical saponin which lathers in water. A cup of fresh leaves, cut and whirled in a blender with two cups of water, makes a good soap substitute. It effectively cleans dishes, yet will safely clean fine laundry as well. The plant spreads faster than it can be used and given slight winter protection, it remains almost evergreen.

Saponaria was formerly thought to remedy skin diseases and, steeped overnight in beer, it was applied to stiff joints and inflammations. It was also said to make a head on beer. New England textile manufacturers cleaned and thickened woolen cloth with bouncing bet in a process called "fulling," accounting for another name, "fuller's herb." The bruised leaves, tied in muslin bags and boiled, made a gentle cleaner for ladies' gloves. More recently, museums have used this herb to clean and restore tapestries and antique fabrics.

Salt Spray Rose

PLATE XVII

PLATE XVIII

Evening-primrose

Bouncing Bet

PLATE XIX

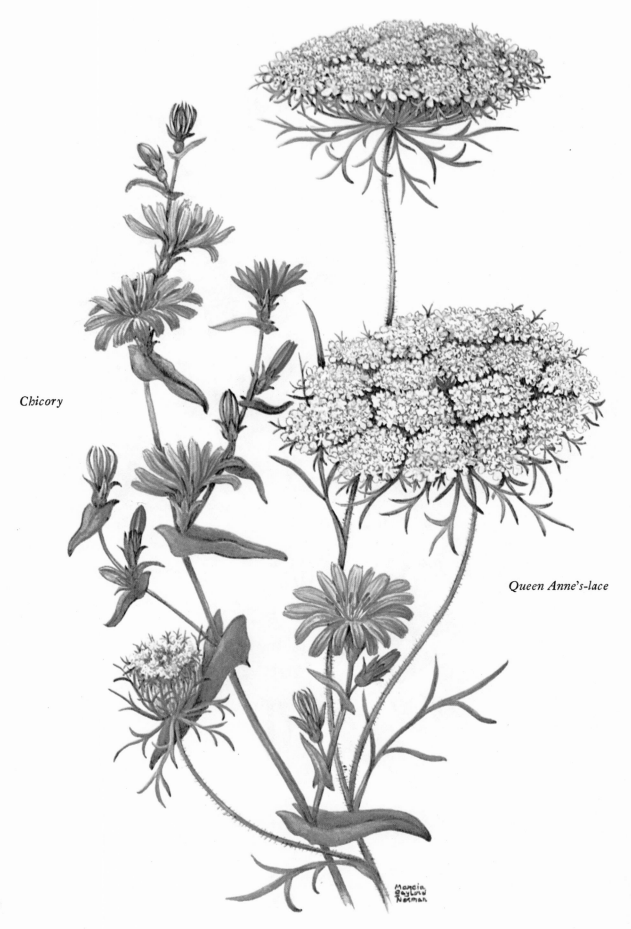

PLATE XX

Chicory

Queen Anne's-lace

MIDSUMMER IS A FIELD OF Queen Anne's-lace spiked with the blue of chicory. In the morning, chicory unfolds a few blossoms of a deep sky blue; as the day progresses, the blue deepens and pink tints bring a lavender tone to the once clear color. By late afternoon the blossom has faded, but no matter— thrifty order portions out the blooms so that ample are left to repeat the show for many days to come. Each lanky stem holds a few buds, blossoms and ripening seed pods simultaneously. The seeds are a favorite food of goldfinches. A meadow dotted with blue chicory and these yellow "wild canaries" presents an enchanting scene of color and bird song.

Herbalists recommended the application of bruised leaves as poultices for inflammations and used the whole plant in the preparation of medicines for liver and kidney disorders. Some old herbals cautioned, however, that overuse might harm the eyesight.

At one time, wild chicory furnished a satisfactory green fodder for sheep and cattle, but retained too much moisture to make good hay. People have found parts of the plant sufficiently to their liking so that an improved variety called witloof or Belgian endive is sold in the markets. To raise the endive in a home garden, sow the seeds in the spring. In the fall, dig the roots, bring them into a cellar and cover them with light soil to a depth of six inches. A pale, blanched leaf head will form after three or four weekly waterings, providing leaves which are fine in a salad or cooked as a potherb. Roasted and ground chicory roots have a long-established reputation as a caffein-free coffee substitute; they may also be used sparingly to flavor soups and stews.

CHICORY
Cichorium Intybus
Family: Composite, Compositae
Flowers: Blue
Blossoms: June—October
Height: 1 to 3 feet
(Plate XX)

A PERSISTENT WEED TO FARMERS, Queen Anne's-lace or wild carrot lifts its filigreed head to join chicory in an extravaganza of blue and white along the wayside.

Queen Anne's-lace, *Daucus Carota*, and the cultivated carrot are of the same species and the latter can revert to its weedy relative. The carrot, probably originating in Afghanistan, was carried to Asia Minor and France in some of its primitive forms. Brought to England by the Dutch, the plant traveled to the New World and was grown in Jamestown in 1609. Its many supposed medicinal qualities accounted for such widespread

QUEEN ANNE'S-LACE
Daucus Carota
Family: Parsley, Umbelliferae
Flowers: White, rarely pink to lavender
Blossoms: June—September
Height: 1 to 4 feet
(Plate XX)

cultivation. Culpeper asserted that the leaves and particularly the seeds were remedies for gravel, dropsy, colic and flatulence. Since he believed the roots caused flatulence, he thankfully noted that the seed "mends what the root marreth."

The large white flower heads frequently have a purple spot in the center, once thought to be poisonous. The lovely umbels attract a host of nectar-hungry insects and the fern-like leaves are food for the caterpillar of the black swallowtail butterfly. Because the flowers become more cup-shaped as the seeds ripen, "bird's nest" is another common name describing the mature umbel.

The flowers, picked before they are fully open, will keep their white color when dried for winter bouquets. Placed in a vase of water tinted with food coloring, the flowers will change almost magically to pastel shades. This is a particularly effective way to teach children the principle of osmosis by which plants are able to obtain water from the soil.

THROUGH ITS LONG HISTORY of usefulness to man, ground ivy has collected many names: "gill-over-the-ground," "cat's foot," "run-away-robin," "hedge-maids" and "Lizzy-run-up-the-hedge." From Saxon times to Henry VIII's reign, the plant was known as "ale hoof" for its use in clarifying and giving bitter flavor to beer. An infusion of the aromatic leaves, "gill tea," was once a popular cough remedy. This bitter drink was also a treatment for jaundice, poisoning, sciatica, gout and the plague. Fresh leaves were bruised and applied to wounds and sores. Early accounts of the antiscorbutic properties of ground ivy may be true; the plant certainly is high in vitamin C content. More recently painters believed it to be a cure for their occupational disease, lead poisoning.

Possessing so many potential virtues, ground ivy, however, remains the most despised weed in suburban America. No other plant invades lawns so successfully. The root is perennial and sends out long runners to produce new plants with small blue-purple flowers which bloom and set seed throughout the summer.

Nevertheless, wherever it can be contained, ground ivy makes a beautiful dark green ground cover. Growing in shady, somewhat damp locations and given good soil, the leaves become almost as large as those of English ivy. Potted and taken indoors in the fall, this weed is transformed into a very satisfactory house plant, particularly good for hanging baskets. A similar ivy with variegated leaves is sold by many nurserymen, but if this, too, is planted outdoors, it will inevitably naturalize and add to the gardener's chores.

QUEEN ANNE'S-LACE
Daucus Carota

GROUND IVY
Glechoma hederacea
Family: Mint, Labiatae
Flowers: Purple-blue
Blossoms: April—July
Height: Up to 6 inches

THE SISTER SHIP OF THE *Mayflower* was christened the *Speed-well*, a fitting name which recalled a tradition of handing fresh blue flowers to travelers with the wish, "Speed well." In time, the words that had so often been associated with the plant became its name. This small herb which so demurely turns its pale petal cup to greet each passerby, would scarcely be thought to have once benefited man. But most of the early herbalists recommend speedwell as a cooling herb and tonic. It served as a treatment for several skin diseases and was an astringent, diaphoretic, alternative and expectorant medicine. It is also reported to be used in the manufacture of some vermouths.

Speedwell, a European native, is now common in the eastern states where it wanders in lawns, gardens and along roadsides. Most varieties are blue, but some nurseries sell white and pink veronica, rarely seen uncultivated. All veronicas enjoy full sun, but occasionally plants will obligingly take to partial shade. The perennial varieties are good choices for rock gardens and borders.

PURSLANE, OR PUSLEY, is a sprawling, prostrate succulent with a preference for blooming in the morning. Gardeners who are familiar with this wild relative of the cultivated portulaca may be surprised to learn that it was once a popular garden plant. While one person may be busily pulling purslane from his garden, his neighbors may be cultivating it as an iron-rich vegetable. The branch tips, or leaves stripped from the stems, are good tossed in salads and the stems can be pickled. Some people dislike the texture of the boiled herb but find it an agreeable addition to soups and gumbo.

Culpeper, combining astrology and medicine, classified purslane under the influence of the moon and labeled it a cooling herb. He was convinced it could cool the blood and lower fevers, cool bruises and, when applied to the forehead, take away "excessive heat therein that hinders rest and sleep."

It may comfort the zealous gardener to note, as he weeds, the interesting pattern of the purslane on the ground—somewhat like a doily.

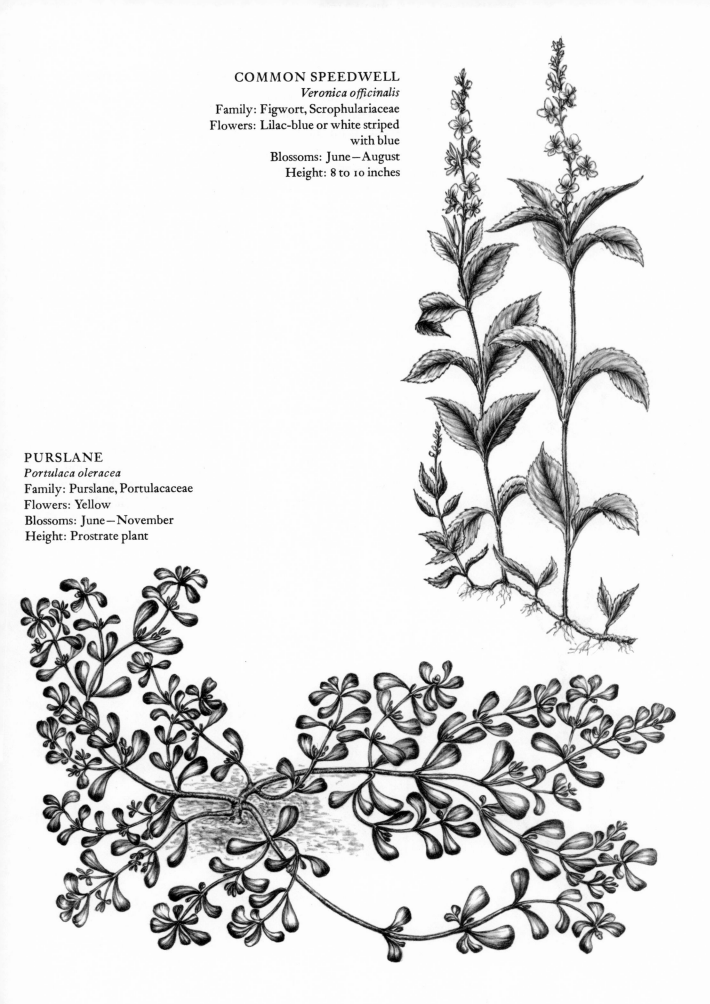

COMMON SPEEDWELL
Veronica officinalis
Family: Figwort, Scrophulariaceae
Flowers: Lilac-blue or white striped
with blue
Blossoms: June—August
Height: 8 to 10 inches

PURSLANE
Portulaca oleracea
Family: Purslane, Portulacaceae
Flowers: Yellow
Blossoms: June—November
Height: Prostrate plant

DAME'S VIOLET
Hesperis matronalis
Family: Mustard, Cruciferae
Flowers: Pink, purple or white
Blossoms: May—August
Height: 2 to 3 feet

THE GREEK ORIGIN OF THE NAME *Hesperis*, meaning "evening star," describes the nocturnally fragrant white-to-rose-purple blossoms of Dame's violet, sometimes called Dame's rocket. Scentless during the day, some flowers hold their perfume until nightfall. By moonlight, a night-scented garden surprises the senses with new hues and shadows, and new fragrances to sweeten the quiet air. Dame's rocket, nicotiana, bouncing bet, evening primrose, sweet woodruff, tuberose and stock all bloom at night and are favorites for the night garden. With the growing popularity of summer outdoor living, these flowers should be treasured for terrace plantings or for containers which may also be brought indoors at dusk for their fragrance.

Dame's rocket was one of Marie Antoinette's favorite plants, known to her as "Julienne des Dames." In her lifetime most gardens had at least a few of these pastel flowers. In England this rocket was aften called the "Whitsun gillyflower," as well as "Dame's violet" and "garden rocket." Having escaped from early gardens where it was cultivated for its fragrance, it has wandered far afield and now deserves to be returned to choice garden spots.

A double white variety was grown in Scotland for over four hundred years. Culpeper mentioned this variety (calling it eveweed) as a cure for wounds, and also described how some people ate it with bread and butter for its garlic-like flavor.

OSWEGO TEA
Monarda didyma
Family: Mint, Labiatae
Flowers: Vermilion
Blossoms: June—August
Height: 2 feet

THE GENUS NAME OF BOTH THESE PLANTS, *Monarda*, honors the distinguished sixteenth-century Spanish botanist and physician, Nicolas Monardes, who wrote numerous works on medicinal and useful herbs, including many from the New World.

Oswego tea, also known as bee balm or red bergamot, is a true American wildflower and like other mints, its native habitats are moist areas and stream banks. At an early date it was introduced into Colonial gardens where it was cherished for its sparkling color. The name bee balm is somewhat misleading as honey bees cannot reach the nectar deep in its tubular flowers; long-tongued bumblebees and butterflies are the pollinators. The vivid red blossoms also attract ruby-throated hummingbirds.

The plant is called Oswego tea after the Oswego Indians who brewed the leaves to make a pungent beverage. When the herb was introduced into England about 1744, some enjoyed this more than the Asian variety. Today's housewife will be rewarded with a new tang to her tea if she adds a few leaves, fresh or dried. The flowers as well as the leaves are delightful in a blend for potpourris. Monarda oil, distilled from several species, is an ingredient in some perfumes but is not to be confused with oil of bergamot extracted from the European bergamot orange.

Wild bergamot grows in drier areas such as thickets, clearings and borders. Its smaller, lilac-colored flowers are very fragrant and a favorite in old-fashioned gardens. More recently several hybrids have been developed with blossoms shading from rose-pink to deep red, yielding long-lasting cut flowers. Their tousled heads are most attractive in bouquets with daisies.

WILD BERGAMOT
Monarda fistulosa
Family: Mint, Labiatae
Flowers: Lilac or pink
Blossoms: July—September
Height: 2 to 3 feet
(Plate XXI)

75

YARROW
Achillea Millefolium
Family: Composite, Compositae
Flowers: White, rarely purplish pink
Blossoms: June—September
Height: 1 to 2 feet
(Plate XXII)

COMMON YARROW TRACES ITS LATIN NAME, *Achillea Mille-folium*, to Greek mythology. Before the siege of Troy the centaur Charon, knowing its healing virtues, gave Achilles this knowledge to heal warriors hurt in battle. Although the plant was named for Achilles, the centaur was not forgotten; bachelor buttons and hawkweed belonging to another group of plants are often called "centaureas." The designation *Millefolium*, meaning "a thousand leaves," refers to the finely cut foliage.

Common yarrow was once called wound-wort or knights' milfoil for its reputation as an important first-aid treatment. Centuries later, herbal doctors still had faith in its healing powers, recommending its use as a tea to induce the perspiration so favored to cleanse the system and cure a bad cold. When the whole plant was boiled and strained, the resulting liquid was one of hundreds of prescriptions for baldness. At one time it was used in Sweden to replace the hops in beer.

The yarrow illustrated here now grows wild, but several others are listed in seed catalogues. Large yellow varieties such as cloth of gold and coronation gold keep their color in dried arrangements. A small relative, *A. tomentosa*, is best suited to rock gardens.

Parents may wish to keep a few plants on hand. When dried and tucked under a young girl's pillow, the aromatic herb will bring her dreams about her future husband. When in due course the young man has been thus identified, the young bride should carry yarrow to the wedding to insure seven happy years.

Wild Bergamot

PLATE XXI

Yarrow

PLATE XXII

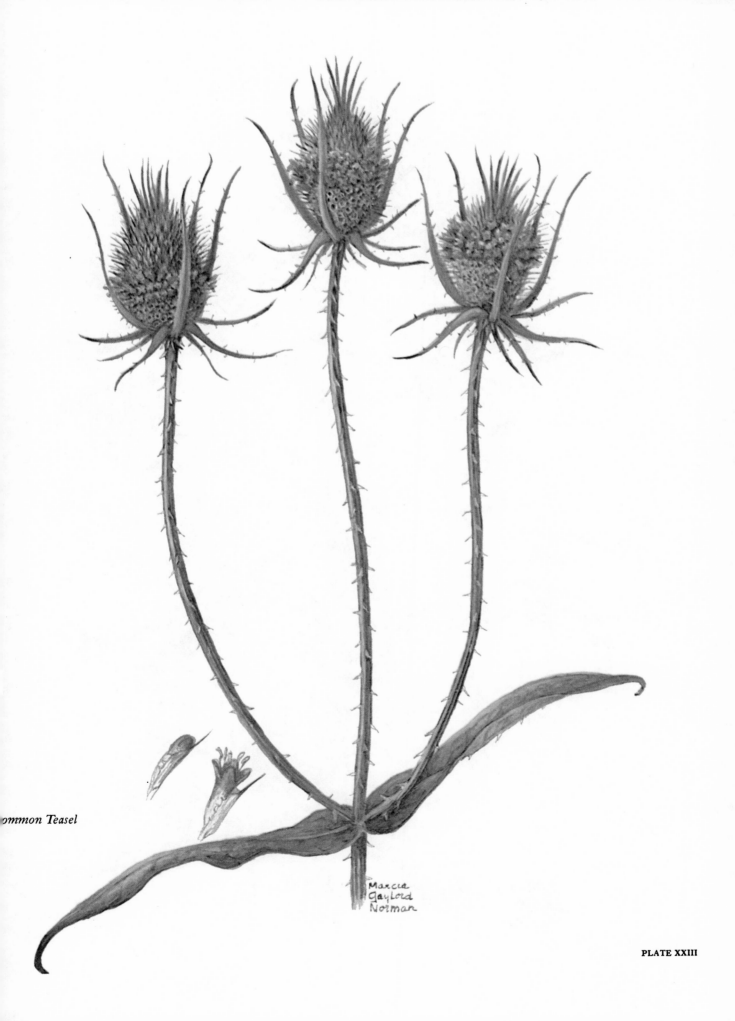

Common Teasel

Marcia
Gaylord
Norman

PLATE XXIII

Boneset

Joe-Pye-weed

PLATE XXIV

COMMON TEASEL AND FULLER'S TEASEL, *Dipsacus fullonum*, are closely related. The most noticeable difference is that the heads of fuller's teasel have hooked spines. There is evidence that it reverts to the common variety; widely distributed in the United States, this European native may be descended from plants grown near woolen mills, because fuller's teasel was sold to textile manufacturers for raising the nap on cloth. The fabric was "teased" without being damaged because the hooks gave way when they became caught. The cultivation of this plant was a serious business. According to Hulme, an acre yielded 160 bushels.

Both varieties were used in primitive medicine. Teasel leaves, at the juncture with the stem, form a small cap which collects dew and rain. The accumulated water was thought to be a cure for warts. Dioscorides, finding that some teasel heads contained worms, advised placing the worms in a pouch to wear around one's neck as an amulet to cure fevers.

Centuries later, Gerard tried this remedy and reported the results in clear terms: "The little worms or maggots, found in the heads of teasel, which are to be hanged about the necke, they are nothing else but most vaine and trifling toies, as myselfe have proved . . . having a most grevous ague, and of long continuance notwithstanding physick charms, these worms hanged about my neck, spiders put into walnutshell and divers such foolish toies that I was constrained to take by phantasticke people's procurement; notwithstanding, I say my help came from God himself, for these medicines, and all other such things, did me no good at all."

Today teasel is filling a new need. With the growing popularity of dried floral arrangements, the decorative form of the blossoming heads makes a most intriguing accent and they are often sold in florist shops for this purpose.

COMMON TEASEL
Dipsacus sylvestris
Family: Teasel, Dipsacaceae
Flowers: Lavender
Blossoms: July—October
Height: 4 to 6 feet
(Plate XXIII)

ONE OF THE PLANTS ILLUSTRATED, *Eupatorium dubium*, is named Joe-Pye-weed for an Indian medicine man of New England who reportedly earned fame and fortune by curing typhus fever and other horrors with this plant. More aptly called queen of the meadow, this beautiful herb towers above goldenrod and wild aster. Nurserymen who now sell wild aster and hybridized goldenrod might do well to offer stately Joe-Pye-weed under a more appealing name. Many herb growers

JOE-PYE-WEED
Eupatorium dubium
Family: Composite, Compositae
Flowers: Magenta
Blossoms: August—September
Height: 3 to 12 feet
(Plate XXIV)

BONESET
Eupatorium perfoliatum
Family: Composite, Compositae
Flowers: White
Blossoms: August—September
Height: 3 to 12 feet
(Plate XXIV)

have transplanted it into their gardens, where it provides a striking display of fall color.

In herbal practice the plant was a substitute for closely related boneset, *E. perfoliatum*; both were used to treat gout and rheumatism. A tea made from boneset was a remedy for an illness that writers in times past called "break bone fever." This may account for the name, since there seems to be minimal connection with the treatment of broken or diseased bones. The disagreeable tasting infusion was served intolerably hot as an emetic for "intermittent fever." It was then administered cold as a restorative tonic for the exhausted patient. An old recipe book suggests another use:

BONESET SYRUP: Take three handfuls [of boneset], put it in a tin basin [of water] and let it stand some time to steep; strain it off, add one pint molasses, and boil it down until quite thick. This is very nice for a bad cough. Take one tablespoonful often.

Another relative in this useful family, *E. hyssopifolium*, or justice weed, is one of countless herbs said to heal insect or snake bites. The latter complaint, in fact, is so often mentioned in old herbals that anyone browsing through them might suspect that snakebite was the major problem our ancestors faced. Both boneset and hyssop-leaved boneset are fine materials for dried flower arrangements. They should be picked before the flowers are completely expanded and hung upside down to dry in a warm, well-ventilated room.

EUPATORIUM
Eupatorium hyssopifolium
Family: Composite, Compositae
Flowers: White
Blossoms: August—September
Height: 3 to 12 feet

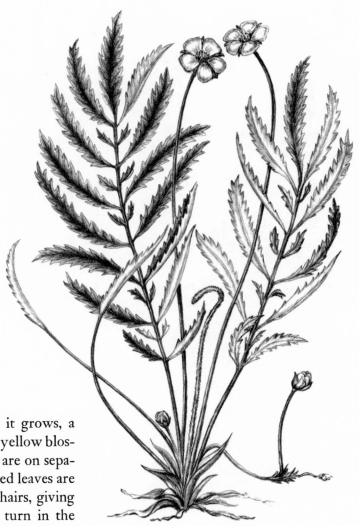

SILVERWEED IS A CHARMING HERB showing, as it grows, a pattern of silver and green sparkled with sunny yellow blossoms. The flowers, like single roses, and the leaves are on separate stems. The upper surfaces of the sharply toothed leaves are green, but the undersides are covered with white hairs, giving them their silvery appearance as they sway and turn in the breeze. Below the leaves and bright blossoms, new plants develop on trailing runners.

The generic name *Potentilla* refers to the potent medicinal qualities attributed to the plant during the Middle Ages. Silverweed was a valued remedy for fevers, laryngitis, toothache, palsy, gout and other conditions. *Anserina*, Latin for "goose," and another common name, goose grass, suggest that geese relish the foliage of this plant above others. The roots are large and sweet enough to be taken as a survival food for man.

Silverweed, like most wild potentillas, can be transplanted into rock gardens and borders. The gardener is cautioned that the plant's delight on reaching new soil knows no bounds. Some varieties have been collected and hybridized. The shrubby cinquefoil, *P. fruticosa*, most clearly reveals its membership in the rose family, rewarding the grower by blossoming almost continuously all summer. Several improved varieties are easily grown as low hedges, also blooming throughout the season. Still others, having three- or five-parted, strawberry-like leaves, produce single or double flowers in shades of rose, orange and yellow.

SILVERWEED
Potentilla anserina
Family: Rose, Rosaceae
Flowers: Yellow
Blossoms: May–September
Height: 1 to 3 feet

THE FINE LEAVES OF THIS PLANT resemble flax; the prefix "toad," however, indicates it is not a true flax and supposedly worthless. Some gardeners will disagree. Toadflax's yellow flowers clearly show that the plant belongs to the snapdragon family and most people know it as butter-and-eggs, a familiar field and roadside weed which is also at home in shady gardens. A toadflax ointment soothed skin irritations and sores. "Lay it in chicken water," Culpeper suggests, "to cure them of the gall; it relieves them when they are drooping." Scandinavians boiled it in milk, then left the milk near windows to attract and poison flies.

Another kind of toadflax, *Cymbalaria muralis*, has become naturalized in a few New England locations. Once known as "ivy-leaved toadflax," the plant puzzles some people, who wonder how snapdragon flowers could grow on an ivy plant. Now called Kenilworth ivy, it is best suited to hanging baskets or chinks in stone walls. Kenilworth ivy was recommended for scurvy and fevers. Sometimes eaten in green salads, it tasted like raw garden peas. Its greatest historic significance, however, was in relation to the science of botany. Carl von Linne, a Swedish naturalist, developed a new system of classifying plants, but when he brought his ideas to the botanic gardens at Oxford he was greeted with skepticism and disapproval for the learned doctors doubted that a man of thirty could challenge the accepted system. One professor, Dillenius, asked his opinion of Kenilworth ivy, a plant which defied botanical classification. Linne's methods solved the riddle by placing it in the figwort family and calling it *Linaria cymbalaria*, now *Cymbalaria muralis*. Dillenius immediately offered to share his house and salary if Linne would be his assistant. When Linne achieved international recognition, his name was Latinized to *Linnaeus*. Today countless plants have scientific names followed by the letter L. to indicate that they were classified by this great botanist.

TOADFLAX
Linaria vulgaris
Family: Figwort, Scrophulariaceae
Flowers: Yellow and orange
Blossoms: June—October
Height: 1 to 3 feet

KENILWORTH IVY
Cymbalaria muralis
Family: Figwort, Scrophulariaceae
Flowers: Pale violet
Blossoms: May—October
Height: Trailing herb

SPOTTED DEAD NETTLE
Lamium maculatum
Family: Mint, Labiatae
Flowers: Rose to purple
Blossoms: April—October
Height: Creeping 8 to 18 inches

TWO HERBS ARE CALLED NETTLES: dead nettles of the mint family, Labiatae, and stinging nettles of the nettle family, Urticaceae. The spotted dead nettle, with a whitish pattern along the mid-rib of its leaves, was introduced from Europe and has escaped from gardens. Red dead nettle, *Lamium purpureum*, and the small weedy henbit, *L. amplexicaule*, have much the same history. In the British Isles all are called archangel, as they blossom each year approximately on the day dedicated to the Archangel Michael. Dead nettles, being smooth, are harmless to touch (and hence the name "dead"), though the shape of their leaves is similar to the stinging nettle. They have the square stems and hooded flowers characteristic of the mint family.

A warming tea was made from the leaves of these nettles to prevent colds. Culpeper recommended them for burns and bruises and for the ability to draw splinters out of the flesh. In reference to one of these plants (though all may be used), he declared, "it makes the heart merry, drives away melancholy, quickens the spirit."

Dead nettles are among the most attractive and satisfactory ground covers for shady areas. If found along the wayside in moist places, they have probably wandered from a nearby garden.

True stinging nettle, *Urtica dioica*, is covered with stiff hairs that sting viciously due to their formic acid content. In years past arthritics were flogged with the plant in the belief that this would relieve their painful disease. This nettle is still an important ingredient in some hair preparations. In Europe the plant was valued as a potherb, but never eaten raw. The young, highly nutritious tips were boiled to prepare a variety of dishes, and they are still used today.

SHEPHERD'S PURSE
Capsella Bursa-pastoris
Family: Mustard, Cruciferae
Flowers: White
Blossoms: April—September
Height: 8 to 18 inches

ALTHOUGH SHEPHERD'S PURSE IS ONE of our most abundant weeds, it is not particularly troublesome for it is shallow-rooted. The Latin name *Capsella*, "little box," and *Bursa-pastoris*, alluding to the shepherd, refer to the similarity of the almost heart-shaped seed pods to the leather pouches once carried by shepherds. The small, four-petaled blossoms on the flower spike develop these conspicuous seed pods on elongated stems.

Shepherd's purse has the pungent taste characteristic of the mustard family. It is a good potherb; the chopped young leaves and stems add variety to salads and the minute seeds are relished by wild birds. The herb's most common medicinal use was for the treatment of hemorrhages, external wounds and sores. "The juice, dropped into the ears, heals the pains, noise and matterings thereof" was Culpeper's graphic description of its cure for an earache.

Peppergrass, *Lepidium virginicum*, looks much like shepherd's purse, but its seed pods are almost disc-shaped. The dried, ground seeds of both plants were among man's first spices and can still be used to make a mustard substitute.

True pepper was once a great luxury. Until about 1800, only the Portuguese knew that it grew in Sumatra and they charged dearly for the scarce condiment. Consequently peppergrass, also called poor man's pepper, was widely used in soups, stews and salads by all but the very wealthy until the nineteenth century.

This little weed is now sought for its decorative effect. If the stalks are cut and dried slightly before maturity, they make a charming filler for dried arrangements; sprayed with a metallic paint, they add sparkle and interest in Christmas decorations.

TANSY, FROM THE GREEK WORD meaning "immortality," was one of the earliest plants brought to the New World. Settlers carefully cultivated it in their gardens as a treasured "simple" or medicinal herb. This sturdy plant has spread beyond their gardens and dooryards to grace our roadsides with its "golden buttons," a most suitable folk name.

Tansy was a household staple filling multiple needs. During the Middle Ages, it was an accepted strewing herb because of its property as an insect repellent and its strong, long-lasting fragrance. Later *The Toilet of Flora*, published in 1799 by an unknown author, advised putting tansy under mattresses or between blankets to combat fleas. The dark green, fern-like leaves were used to protect meat from flies and clothing from moths.

The medicinal properties of tansy were recognized by herbalists who prescribed it for rheumatism, gout, jaundice, dyspepsia and occasional hysteria, and were grateful that it had always been available in plenty for all its applications. An infusion of the leaves formerly made a bitter spring tonic, but because of its potent medicinal properties the plant may be considered too dangerous for internal use. In small quantities, however, it was used as a flavoring for tansy puddings. Snippets of the herb combined with eggs, bread crumbs, cream, sugar, butter and spinach juice were the ingredients mentioned in most recipes.

Though an old-fashioned plant, tansy is still suitable for modern gardens where its deep-colored, finely cut foliage and flat heads of button-sized yellow blossoms add welcome form and color. Of course it should be included in the herb garden, but the gardener will want to thin the new plants forming from the creeping roots to keep them within bounds. The bright blossoms are very long-lasting and remain a cheerful yellow when dried, keeping them in great demand by flower arrangers.

TANSY
Tanacetum vulgare
Family: Composite, Compositae
Flowers: Golden yellow
Blossoms: July—September
Height: 18 to 30 inches
(Plate XXV)

THE ARTEMISIAS FORM A CONFUSING group of plants named for Artemis, Greek goddess of the moon and the chase, as well as guardian of women and children. These herbs became symbols of health, and physicians painted them on their doors to advertise their profession. Perhaps some of the lore of *Artemisia vulgaris* grew out of the association of Artemis with the hunt and with wild animals for it was put into amulets by travelers to dissolve fatigue and drive away beasts and devils. Some energetic travelers placed mugwort in their shoes with the ambitious idea of walking forty miles before noon without tiring.

Although in medieval lore the plant was linked to John the Baptist, it never lost its earlier magical associations. Gathered by

COMMON MUGWORT
Artemisia vulgaris
Family: Composite, Compositae
Flowers: Yellowish green
Blossoms: July—October
Height: 1 to 3 feet
(Plate XXVI)

the full of the moon and worn around one's neck, the herb was supposed to drive away "fanatical spirits." Culpeper claimed that mugwort was excellent for female disorders and helped to hasten delivery of a baby. It was also prescribed for sciatica, epilepsy, tape worm and overindulgence in opium.

Housewives have found various uses for this pungent herb. For centuries, for example, it has been used to repel moths. A pleasant closet sachet can be made by blending the following:

SACHET

6 cups dried cut tansy	½ cup cinnamon stick, crushed
6 cups dried cut mint	½ cup whole cloves, crushed
5 cups dried cut santolina	½ cup orris root
4 cups dried cut mugwort	½ dram clove oil

The name mugwort reflects its use in brewing before hops were known in England. A closely related plant, *A. Absinthium*, imparted its bitter flavor to the dangerous liquor, absinthe. Classified as a weed by many, mugwort is familiar along the roadsides. Its typical artemisia leaves, rather coarsely cut, show an interesting contrast of deep green on top and soft gray beneath.

SWEET GOLDENROD
Solidago odora
Family: Composite, Compositae
Flowers: Golden yellow
Blossoms: July—September
Height: 2 to 3 feet
(Plate XXVI)

DURING THE AMERICAN REVOLUTION, sweet goldenrod took the place of the English tea which the patriots had misplaced in Boston. The anise-flavored beverage was called Blue Mountain tea. Indians brewed a stronger infusion from Canadian goldenrod, gargling with it for sore throats. This species and others were also a popular source of yellow dye.

Although many goldenrods are found in America, only one is native to Great Britain. Gerard wrote that imported goldenrod easily sold for a crown an ounce. The herb was thought to be a diuretic, tonic and astringent, but after it was discovered growing wild in Hempstead Wood, it was rarely prescribed. This caused Gerard to reflect upon the proverb: "Far fetcht and deare bought is best for Ladies." This, he wrote, might apply better to physicians who disregarded easily obtained medicines, physicians who sought new cures farther away, and "many times hurt more than they helpe."

Because goldenrods grow so abundantly by our roadsides, they have been almost overlooked by gardeners. There are several cultivated varieties, however, which can add brilliant color to a late summer border. There is no need to worry about their causing hay fever because ragweed, not goldenrod, is usually the cause of that distress. Most goldenrod flowers will keep their sunny color if picked and hung to dry before they are fully open.

Tansy

PLATE XXV

Sweet Goldenrod

Common Mugwort

PLATE XXVI

Quack Grass

Bindweed

PLATE XXVII

Pokeweed

PLATE XXVIII

Q̲ᴜᴀᴄᴋ ɢʀᴀss, ᴡʜᴏsᴇ Lᴀᴛɪɴ ɴᴀᴍᴇ, *Agropyron repens*, means "creeping field wheat," is most unwelcome in lawns and gardens, but it was not always considered worthless. Also commonly called "couch grass" and "witch grass," the seeds were fed to caged birds, and cattle grazed on its new growth and ate hay cut from the blossoming grass. The reputed medicinal value applied to a wide range of ailments. Once a favorite herbal remedy for kidney disorders, the dried roots are still sold by botanical supply houses. A root infusion produced a popular spring tonic.

Gardeners hold quack grass in less esteem, for the underground network of creeping rhizomes makes it most difficult to eradicate. Since the roots have phenomenal regenerative properties, even the smallest toothpick-sized root left in the ground will grow new plants.

It is wasted effort to sow any kind of seeds in ground infested with quack grass, with the exception of pumpkins or gourds whose broad leaves shade and weaken the grass. A gardener who lacks time for painstaking weeding can set out tomato or cabbage plants with some anticipation of success. That failing, however, he can at least be confident that he will never go hungry because quack grass roots may be dried and ground into meal for baking bread.

QUACK GRASS
Agropyron repens
Family: Grass, Gramineae
Flowers: Green
Blossoms: May—September
Height: 1 to 3 feet
(Plate XXVII)

B̲ɪɴᴅᴡᴇᴇᴅ ᴏʀ ʜᴇᴅɢᴇ ʙɪɴᴅᴡᴇᴇᴅ, *Convolvulus sepium*, from *convolvere*, "to entwine," and *sepes*, "a hedge," is a twining plant that quickly wraps itself around its neighbors, usually turning in a counter-clockwise direction. This close relative of the morning glory has a spiral twist of buds which open into white or light pink striped trumpets in the sun, but remain closed on gray days. It is scorned as a weed because its tight embrace strangles other plants and its extensive root system depletes the soil; but it is forgiven when one sees it quickly covering some unsightly spot with its lovely bloom.

Like other members of the convolvulus family, bindweed was considered a purgative and was so used in herbal medicine. Today, bindweed can be planted to trail over walls and fences where there is sufficient room to ramble without causing damage.

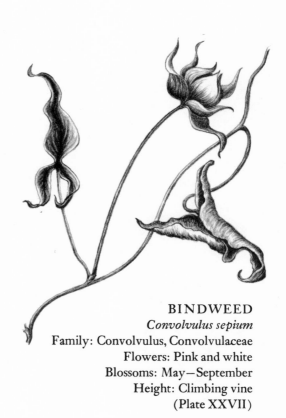

BINDWEED
Convolvulus sepium
Family: Convolvulus, Convolvulaceae
Flowers: Pink and white
Blossoms: May—September
Height: Climbing vine
(Plate XXVII)

IN MAY, RED CLOVER SPREADS a rose-red tablecloth for bumble-bees. Honeybees wait until second growth appears to gather nectar from the shorter tubes. When New Zealanders imported red clover to their continent, they neglected to import bumble-bees and so harvested no seed the first season. Red clover was first brought to America as a hay crop, a use that remains important today. American Indians sometimes dried the roots for food but more often boiled the whole herb or cooked it between hot stones.

Old medicinal books listed red clover as an "alternative;" a plant that slowly improves a person's health. The herb, so easily obtained, made a quieting tea to soothe nerves or relieve coughs and was a popular treatment for countless other disorders.

Today the several species of clover are associated with the special flavor the nectar imparts to honey. All the clovers, like other legumes, are rich in nitrogen and nourish the lawns in which they grow to a verdant green.

PARTS OF POKEWEED ARE POISONOUS; the roots and seeds are the most dangerous, as well as any stems that have grown large enough to be tinged with purple. The herb was used as an ingredient in an ointment to treat skin diseases and arthritis, and as a substitute for the emetic, ipecac. The drug trade once purchased large roots in quantity, an acre yielding six hundred pounds. Nowadays, a patent arthritis remedy still contains pokeweed.

Juice from the berries colored cake frosting and wine. In fact, some Portuguese vintners deceived their customers by tinting inferior wines with this juice until a law was passed to prohibit the cutting of this introduced American plant. Birds eat the berries to build up strength for their fall migrations. An old name, "pigeon-berry," is a reminder that pokeberries were a favorite food of the now-extinct passenger pigeons. Young pokeweed shoots, when no more than four or five inches long, make a delicious vegetable. An Arkansas cannery sells them under the name "poke sallet."

In late summer pokeweed, called a rank weed by some, presents a handsome display of contrasting colors. The tall stems are a clear red purple; the midveins of the smooth green leaves are tinted like the stem; and the terminal, loose flower spire frequently has the white blossoms and berries.

RED CLOVER
Trifolium pratense
Family: Pulse, Leguminosae
Flowers: Rose to magenta
Blossoms: May—September
Height: 8 to 24 inches

POKEWEED
Phytolacca americana
Family: Pokeweed, Phytolaccaceae
Flowers: White
Blossoms: July—September
Height: 4 to 10 feet
(Plate XXVIII)

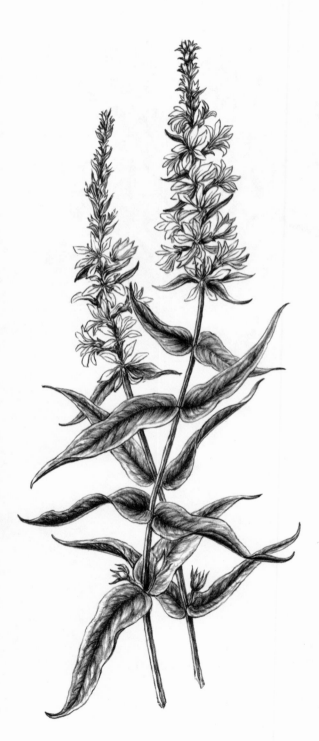

B ROUGHT HERE FROM EUROPE, spiked or purple loosestrife has found a congenial habitat along streams and in our swamps and wet meadows, where it forms large areas of such brilliant color that it attracts even the attention of speeding motorists. The gaudy, magenta-red flowers are borne on long tapering spikes that have been carefully studied by botanists and naturalists, including Charles Darwin. The blossoms were found to be trimorphous, that is, to have three distinct forms of flowers, with only one kind on each plant. In this case, the differences are in the lengths of the stamens and styles, which are varied in their relationship so as to guarantee cross fertilization.

Herbal books report that loosestrife relaxed the stress of nervous disorders, which may account for its common name. A distillation was applied to bruised or sore eyes, and it was often gargled in warm water for throat irritations. The herb was also used in the process of tanning leather.

Yellow loosestrife, *Lysimachia vulgaris*, is a member of the primrose family and is related to spiked loosestrife in name only. The Latin name may have honored King Lysimachus of Thrace, who once was supposedly chased by an enraged bull. Grasping a loosestrife, he waved the plant before the bull which immediately became calm and quiet. Perhaps this tale accounts for the old saying that if this plant were thrown between quarreling oxen, they would separate. Tied to their yokes, it stopped trouble before it began.

SPIKED LOOSESTRIFE
Lythrum Salicaria
Family: Loosestrife, Lythraceae
Flowers: Magenta
Blossoms: June – September
Height: 2 to 3 feet

COMMON ELDER
Sambucus canadensis
Family: Honeysuckle, Caprifoliaceae
Flowers: White
Fruit: Purplish black
Blossoms: June—July
Height: Shrub to 7 feet

COLONISTS, UPON THEIR ARRIVAL in America, soon recognized one of their oldest medicinal sources, the common elder. Their familiar European elder tree reaches heights of over thirty feet, but the American plant is not so tall and, growing in dense thickets, is generally called an elderberry bush. Centuries ago superstitious fears kept many people from trimming elder but contemporary gardeners should not hesitate because the bushes grow so luxuriantly in damp soil that berry picking is often nearly impossible.

A Danish story tells of the elder-tree mother, Hylde-Moer, who guarded each tree. Her permission had to be asked before any wood was cut, but silence was always the affirmative answer. A Dane wishing to meet the Elfin King and his court needed only to stand beneath an elder tree on Midsummer's Eve. Folklore in other countries credited the elder with magical protective powers. Peasants fashioned crosses from the twigs, placing them over stable doors to keep their animals secure, and planted elder trees near their houses to keep out witches.

Traditionally the flowers, berries and roots of elder were considered medicinal and were used to treat over seventy different diseases. The distilled flowers make a cleansing lotion which can be applied to restore sunburned and freckled skin. Elder blossoms as well as berries are used to make the familiar country wine.

IN TIMES PAST IT WAS CUSTOMARY to extract medicines from water lilies. Culpeper suggested that the flowers be made into a syrup which would procure rest and settle the brains of frantic persons. Herbalists considered the roots an astringent and found them to be a storehouse of tannin, starch, ammonia and other useful substances. It was inevitable that someone living near a mosquito-infested swamp would try the handy lily pads as a cooling poultice; subsequently they became known to herbalists as an anodyne, a pain reliever. Weavers in the Hebrides gathered water lilies for a black dye. After crushing the roots and adding water, they boiled them until the liquid became dark brown, adding copper to further darken the dye.

The strikingly beautiful white or pinkish flowers with their sweet fragrance and familiar round lily pads, green on top, purplish underneath, are the essence of a quiet pond. Blossoms appear in the morning and close in the afternoon. The seed pods are not visible among the lily pads because after pollination the flower stem sinks below the surface to develop its seeds under water.

Although seemingly plentiful in some areas, water lilies are best left undisturbed for all to enjoy. In many wild areas, ponds become so crowded with lily pads that it is necessary to pick up a leaf to see the water. Anyone unable to resist the temptation to pick these flowers must be careful not to pull up the roots. A gardener transplanting water lilies to his own pool should do so in the spring. They will grow best if planted in rich soil, then covered with at least two feet of water; propagation may be by root division or seed.

WATER LILY
Nymphaea odorata
Family: Water Lily, Nymphaeaceae
Flowers: White
Blossoms: June–September

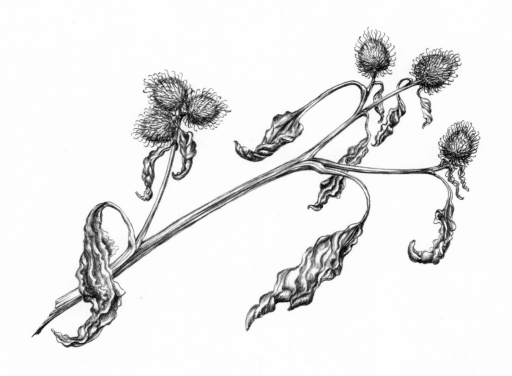

BURDOCK IS EASILY RECOGNIZED by its head of bristly, tenacious burrs which cling to every passing creature; its genus name, *Arctium*, is derived from the Greek word *arctos*, meaning a bear. A symbiotic relationship develops with animals who distribute the seeds for the plant they may later feed upon. Burdock is a problem for sheep farmers because the burrs become snarled in the fleece and lower the quality of the wool. A tall coarse weed, the thistle-like blossoms are an exquisite and rewarding sight to anyone who inspects them closely with an unprejudiced eye.

Countless medicinal properties were attributed to burdock; most of them related to skin or kidney ailments, but it was also used for rheumatism. Culpeper offers a tempting remedy for one serious illness; he stated that the herb drunk with wine for forty days should "wonderfully help sciatica."

The gardener who is intent on digging out this weed should save some of the stalks because, if collected before the plant flowers, they make an acceptable vegetable. After the stalks are peeled, they should be boiled, drained and boiled again. The Japanese cultivate a variety called "gobo."

BURDOCK
Arctium Lappa
Family: Composite, Compositae
Flowers: Light magenta purple
Blossoms: July—October
Height: 4 to 8 feet
(Plate XXIX)

YELLOW DOCK
Rumex crispus
Family: Buckwheat, Polygonaceae
Flowers: Green
Blossoms: June—August
Height: 1 to 4 feet
(Plate XXX)

RABBITS, ALTHOUGH THEY SHARE with humans an appreciation of garden vegetables, do not seek carrots or lettuce as a first choice but, surprisingly, prefer dock—a good reason for leaving a few dock plants near one's garden. This plant is sometimes called "curled dock," because of its twisting leaves. They can be prepared and cooked like spinach, while the roots can be dug and the blanched greens forced in a cellar in the manner of Belgian endive.

Dock seed heads are the most conspicuous part of the plant. They may be picked and dried for flower arrangements in several stages of development, each having its own color variations. Children have discovered that the fully ripe brown seeds look like coffee grounds and are just right for make-believe. American Indians pounded the seeds into meal, and used the roots medicinally. After a long winter spent preparing dried, pickled or salted foods, Colonial housewives must have felt some relief upon seeing this early spring green. In herbal medicine, dock was known as a blood purifier, while a dried root infusion was taken for liver disorders. Fresh roots were mascerated, mixed with lard and applied to skin irritations.

Dock, of Eurasian origin, is now a weed and has several species, all of which are tall, rather handsome plants that should be admired for their beauty. In the fall, the distinctive forms of the winged fruit identify the species and disclose an intricate network pattern (reticulation) when observed through a hand lens.

Burdock

PLATE XXIX

PLATE XXX

Yellow Dock

Blackberry

Marcia
gaylord
Norman

PLATE XXXI

Staghorn Sumac

PLATE XXXII

THE BLACKBERRY'S THORNY THICKETS and arches protect young trees from deer and hungry farm animals and at the same time shelter smaller animals from predators. Berry pickers would do well to wear heavily protective clothing. A person working by himself must be industrious if he is to pick enough berries to try this seventeenth-century recipe:

TO MAKE BLACKBURY WINE: Take one Bushell of Blackburys, nine quarts of water, six pounds of sugar; boyle your water and sugar together; then bruize your blackburys in a marble mortar; when they be cold put them together and let them stand 24 hours; then put it into a vessell that will fill and let it stand one month, and then if it be clear bottle it off.

The berries make delicious shortcake, jellies and jams. Home-canned blackberries are a treat and most appreciated in the late winter when fruit in the market is scarce or unappetizing.

The leaves and root bark were used in folk medicine because they contain tannin which was responsible for their reputation as an astringent. Gerard said, "The leaves of Bramble boyled in water, with honey, allum, and a little white wine added thereto, make a most excellent lotion or washing water, and the same decoction fastneth the teeth."

In early summer one notes the abundance of the white, five-petaled blossoms that grace the arching canes in anticipation of the autumnal harvest of the purple-black, ripe berries to be picked and eaten still warm from the sun.

BLACKBERRY
Rubus species
Family: Rose, Rosaceae
Flowers: White or roseate
Fruit: Purplish black
Blossoms: May—July
Height: Shrub 3 to 6 feet
(Plate XXXI)

STAGHORN SUMAC
Rhus typhina
Family: Cashew, Anacardiaceae
Flowers: Whitish
Fruit: Red
Blossoms: June—July
Height: Shrub 3 to 10 feet
(Plate XXXII)

THE PRESENCE OF STAGHORN SUMAC is an indication of poor soil and a signal to prospective farm buyers to look further, perhaps until they find land which supports, instead, a healthy stand of thistles. The magnificent crimson foliage and terminal fuzzy red fruit clusters, however, are among the most colorful autumn roadside displays. Indians collected and stored the torch-shaped fruit to make a citrus-like beverage for winter. In folk medicine, the berries were boiled and the liquid cooled and gargled for sore throats.

Smooth sumac, *Rhus glabra*, is a similar but smaller shrub. The red berries appear smooth although they are covered with minute hairs which contain malic acid, possibly accounting for another name, "vinegar tree." A pleasant beverage similar to lemonade can be made by covering the berries with water, crushing them, then straining the liquid carefully. Staghorn sumac berries are equally good for this. Smooth sumac bark made tonic, astringent and antiseptic medicines. The roots yielded a yellow dye; the berries a black one. At one time, the plant was cultivated for the leaves and bark which were utilized in tanning leather and dyeing wool.

Beware of the poison sumac, *R. Vernix*, as well as the notorious poison ivy, *R. radicans*; both are readily identified by their whitish berries. Fortunately this dangerous sumac is usually inaccessible, growing deep in swampy thickets, but the scarlet foliage is attractive in the fall and has caused cases of severe dermatitis to those unwise enough to pick it.

THERE ARE OVER FORTY VARIETIES OF *Polygonum* listed in Gray's *Manual of Botany*, including the closely related group of smartweeds. The pink-flowered Lady's-thumb, illustrated here, grows abundantly in damp locations in gardens, fields, along roadsides and the shore. This tall plant with its rather lax habit of growth attracts attention by its compact rosy-pink flower spikes. Juice extracted from Lady's-thumb treated cuts, wounds, and bruises. In our southern mountain regions, it was eaten as an early salad green.

Very similar in appearance, common smartweed or water-pepper, *P. Hydropiper*, is more slender and has pale green flowers. As the name implies, the plant is very acid and peppery. Water-pepper was a valuable dye herb, the source of a durable yellow color for wool. When dried, the herb reportedly repelled moths. Culpeper claimed that a person need only strew common smartweed in a room and all the fleas would be killed. A handful of this useful plant tucked beneath a saddle was thought to keep a horse from becoming hungry or thirsty.

SMOOTH SUMAC
Rhus glabra
Family: Cashew, Anacardiaceae
Flowers: Whitish; fruit: red
Blossoms: June—July
Height: Shrub, 2 to 10 feet

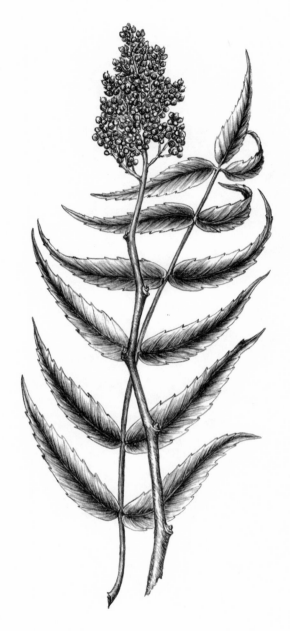

LADY'S-THUMB
Polygonum Persicaria
Family: Buckwheat, Polygonaceae
Flowers: Crimson pink
Blossoms: June—October
Height: 6 to 24 inches

JERUSALEM ARTICHOKE
Helianthus tuberosus
Family: Composite, Compositae
Flowers: Golden yellow
Blossoms: August—October
Height: 1 to 8 feet

JERUSALEM ARTICHOKE IS REALLY a sunflower, although the unopened buds reportedly can be boiled and eaten like globe artichokes. Champlain, after being told by the Indians that artichoke tubers were edible, took the plants back to France. Since then they have been better known in Europe than in the United States. In 1629, John Parkinson wrote that they were so common in London that "even the vulgar began to despise them."

As with so many of our fruits and vegetables, taste and nutrition are sometimes valued less than shipping qualities, and this may explain why Jerusalem artichokes are not more readily available in markets. Peeled, sliced and eaten raw in salads, the tubers have the delightful crispness of water chestnuts and taste like coconut. Their flavor when baked or boiled is subtle. Health food stores carry a variety of Jerusalem artichoke products because they are starch-free. The tubers contain inulin and are used to make noodles, macaroni and other foods for people on restricted diets. A few plants started in the back of a garden quickly form a large patch, insuring a never-ending supply of these nutritious tubers. We have dug out an entire bed of artichokes, only to have even more growing in the same spot the following year.

Other sunflowers also have herbal properties. Common sunflower, *Helianthus annuus*, smaller than the garden varieties, holds a medicinal oil in its seeds which was given for coughs and laryngitis. Sunflower oil, however, has been most often used in the manner of olive oil for cooking. American colonists boiled the seeds to release the oil, a method they learned from the Indians. Stem fibers were used to make paper and the flowers yielded a superior yellow dye. The seeds of this and *H. giganteus* were roasted and ground to make flour which was sometimes mixed with cornmeal.

WILD SARSAPARILLA IS MOST NOTICEABLE in the autumn when the relatively inconspicuous white flowers have been replaced by the clusters of purple-black berries which contrast sharply with the golden leaves. This plant is unusual in its growth pattern because the flower and leaf stems separate just above the root. The solitary, long leaf stem terminates in three divisions, each bearing five oval pointed leaflets.

Found in rich, moist woods, the aromatic horizontal roots of wild sarsaparilla have been widely sought in the past as a substitute for the true sarsaparilla, *Smilax officinalis*, which grows in warm climates. Some herbalists disputed the medicinal value of the American plant but Dr. O. Phelps Brown and others thought it might be equal or superior to the imported varieties. It was considered anti-rheumatic and pectoral and thought to be an alternative, acting slowly to generally improve the patient's condition. The aromatic rootstock was collected in the fall to be used in medicinal preparations and as a flavoring in some carbonated beverages. As is the case with so many modern flavorings, sarsaparilla is now likely to be synthetic.

Wild sarsaparilla closely resembles ginseng, *Panax quinquefolius*, belonging to the same plant family, ginseng. This relatively rare plant has long been esteemed by the Chinese for its potent medicinal values. It is probably scarce because it has been so excessively collected to meet the export demand.

WILD SARSAPARILLA
Aralia nudicaulis
Family: Ginseng, Araliaceae
Flowers: Greenish white
Blossoms: May–July
Height: 7 to 15 inches

VIRGINIA CREEPER
Parthenocissus quinquefolia
Family: Vine, Vitaceae
Flowers: Whitish green
Fruit: Bright blue
Flowers: June—August
Height: Creeping vine

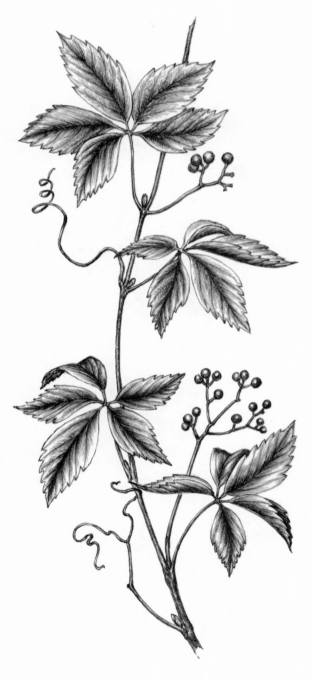

THIS HARMLESS VINE IS OFTEN MISTAKEN for poison ivy, although one can readily see that the leaves of Virginia creeper have five lobes, while those of poison ivy have three. It is a handsome vine with bright blue berries, climbing with the aid of adhesive disks on the branched tendrils. In fall its color is radiant; vines often reach the tops of trees, beautifully exhibiting their poinsettia-red leaves against a green background.

Native to America and taken from Canada to Europe, Virginia creeper, sometimes called American ivy, was cultivated there by the early seventeenth century. Parkinson, in whose lifetime it was introduced, described it at some length, noting the crumpled or folded appearance of the young leaves, red at first, then becoming green.

The berries were used as a treatment for fever and as an antiseptic during the Great Plague in London. According to Dr. Brown, "An old author affirms that there is a very great antipathy between wine and ivy, and therefore it is a remedy to preserve against drunkenness, and to relieve or cure intoxication by drinking a draught of wine in which a handful of bruised ivy leaves have been boiled."

Formerly the plants were considered a benefit to the body from head to toe, not only destroying lice but also easing the pain of corns and bunions. The boiled leaves can furnish a black dye. Today it is grown as a decorative vine, climbing high on buildings or along stone walls.

WHITE SASSAFRAS
Sassafras albidum
Family: Laurel, Lauraceae
Flowers: Greenish yellow
Blossoms: April—June
Height: Tree 15 to 50 feet

According to Mrs. Grieve, "Oil of Sassafras was chiefly used for flavoring purposes, particularly to conceal the flavor of opium when given to children." This shocking treatment was doubly dangerous; the oil, no longer used in beverages, contains safrole, now known to have induced malignant tumors in laboratory animals. At one time, however, tea made from the roots was thought to cure rheumatism and fevers.

Fossil evidence proves that sassafras grew in Europe until the last glacial period when it became extinct there. In 1606, when Bartholomew Gosnold's party of explorers went ashore on the Elizabeth Islands off the coast of Massachusetts, one of his companions discovered sassafras growing abundantly. The plant's supposed medicinal qualities were already well known to the Indians. Although Spanish explorers had evidently introduced it to Europe at an earlier date, quantities of sassafras roots were subsequently collected and taken to England where it was valued both as a new medicinal discovery and simply as a good tasting tea.

Filet powder, a seasoning and thickening for gumbo, is made from the powdered leaves. Even if the culinary uses are discontinued, sassafras oil will probably continue to scent soaps and perfumes. Sassafras is worth planting if only to attract the beautiful tiger swallowtail butterfly, who searches it out and lays her eggs on the leaves, thus assuring the proper food for her young. The tree is an interesting oddity because it may have three kinds of leaves on one twig: some are simple, while others look like mittens or have three lobes.

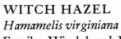

WITCH HAZEL
Hamamelis virginiana
Family: Witch hazel, Hamamelidaceae
Flowers: Yellow
Blossoms: September–November
Height: Shrub, 10 to 12 feet

SWEET FERN
Comptonia peregrina
Family: Wax-Myrtle, Myricaceae
Flowers: Green to brown
Blossoms: April–June
Height: Shrub 1 to 2 feet

FOUND IN OPEN, DAMP WOODS, witch hazel is an eccentric shrub or small tree. In the fall, after it has lost its leaves, it produces yellow flowers notable for the four long, curling, strap-like petals. At the same time, the seed capsule from the previous year ripens, splits open and forcibly ejects its seeds. Thus each twig bears three generations: the developing winter bud, the flower and the ripe seed pod. This characteristic, as well as its habit of late blooming, makes it an interesting landscape plant. The smooth, very dark brown bark is mottled with lighter brown, explaining an Indian name meaning "spotted stick."

This wood has an unusual place in history; dowsers paced across our lands clutching forked branches of witch hazel hoping to find water or minerals. The European hazel was also used for divining and was believed to be especially successful when carried by "wise women" or witches; hence the name witch hazel.

The Indians are credited with the discovery of yet another use for the bark and twigs, leading to the development of a lotion which may be more familiar than the shrub. One Connecticut family has manufactured Witch Hazel Lotion for four generations, selling it to drug stores and barber shops. The label recommends it for bruises, bites, stings, sunburn, mouth wash and gargles, and for muscular stiffness. It is an astringent aftershave lotion and, when chilled, an invigorating skin freshener.

SWEET FERN, DESPITE ITS COLLOQUIAL NAME, is distinguished from true ferns because it is really a low shrub and prefers to grow in clearings in dry, sunny locations instead of in rich, damp soil. The generic name, *Comptonia*, honors a seventeenth-century Bishop of London, Henry Compton, who was an enthusiastic botanist and plant collector.

The fragrant leaves of mature plants can be picked after the first fall frost, dried and sewn into sachets. In linen closets and drawers, their refreshing sweetness is never musky or cloying. According to M. L. Fernald, during June and July country children shelled the sweet fern burrs to eat the tender nutlets. The shelling process usually required using a thumbnail which inevitably was stained yellow by the resinous oil. A leaf infusion was a trusted cure for poison ivy rash and the same palatable infusion, or tea, was said to promote perspiration and relieve stomach distress. Sweet fern also has astringent properties.

OLD MAN'S BEARD GROWS EITHER ERECT or hanging on oak and evergreen branches, providing ready-made nests for Parula warblers who rearrange it to suit their needs. A few lichens, including *Usnea*, add their fragrant components to many of the choice, long-lasting modern perfumes. The fragrance of the lichen varies with the growing conditions and the type of host tree, therefore it is advisable to test a batch before mixing sachets or potpourris that contain old man's beard. Medicinally the plant once served as a tonic and diuretic as well as an ingredient in hair-care preparations.

All the great variety of lichens growing on trees or among the woodland pine needles are seen at their best after a spell of rain or during foggy days when the moisture brings out the shades of green and gray in contrast to the darkened bark of the wet trees. One of the advantages of lichens from a collector's standpoint is their availability throughout the year, making them ideal subjects for winter botanizing. Charming small wreaths five or six inches in diameter can be made on a wire frame covered with crushed paper and burlap strips. Various lichens, dried seed pods and acorns are tucked into the wrapped burlap or glued in place. Adding a small red or green velvet bow transforms them into Christmas decorations.

OLD MAN'S BEARD
Usnea florida
Lichen
Color: Greenish gray with buff fruits
Present throughout the year
Height: Growing on trees, 2 inches

WHEN ALGAE AND FUNGUS FORM a symbiotic relationship, the resulting combination is called a lichen. The algae contains chlorophyll, enabling it to produce carbohydrates to nourish the fungus, which stores moisture and furnishes inorganic materials.

Large patches of gray-green reindeer moss often blanket poor, acid soil in pine woods and serve to build humus, thus providing enrichment for future generations of plant growth. Lichens may appear deceptively worthless, but they have proved valuable for centuries; usnic acid, nowadays derived from this lichen, is a prime ingredient of a healing salve. Since the time of the Pharaohs, Egyptians have made lichen bread, a survival food. A nutritious jelly can be made by boiling and then straining reindeer moss to obtain a liquid which will jell when cool. In the nineteenth century, a Swedish distillery transformed the lichen into brandy. Forest floors were quickly stripped of the moss because the enterprise was so successful; the practice had to be discontinued for lack of raw material. This lichen serves as winter forage for the reindeer of northern countries.

REINDEER MOSS
Cladonia rangiferina
Lichen
Color: Silvery gray, brown fruits on tips
Present throughout the year
Height: 2 to 4 inches

COMMON REED
Phragmites communis
Family: Grass, Gramineae
Flowers: Tawny
Blossoms: July—September
Height: 4 to 12 feet

BEFORE THE SEVENTH CENTURY, writing pens were made from the common reed, but at that time they were replaced by quills, although reeds continued to be important for many other purposes. In Southern France, on the Isle de la Camarague, the inhabitants once built their houses of reed. Today they thatch their roofs with it, and the wild white horses of the region eat the tender shoots. Seafaring men have called it "horse grass" (doubtless referring to the size of the plant) in much the same way that they have called tuna "horse mackerel." Duck hunters weave the supple green reeds through chicken wire to make lightweight, portable blinds.

Early in the season before they blossom, the reeds are full of starch and sugar. Indians dried and pounded them into a powder which they moistened and browned by the fire to make a sticky confection. They ate the seeds as gruel. Underground shoots are delicious pickled. The plumes can be used to dye woolen cloth green, but they are more likely to be dried for winter bouquets. They can be shaped into Christmas wreaths, but unless sprayed with gold or other colored paint, the result may appear to have been made from fur. Common reed's mass of roots serves an important ecological function, binding the soil along marshes and preventing erosion.

Bibliography

Adrosko, Rita J. *Natural Dyes and Home Dyeing.* U. S. National Museum Bulletin 281, 1968; New York: Dover Publications, Inc., 1971.

Anderson, A. A. *How We Got Our Flowers.* William & Norgate, Ltd. under title "The Coming of Flowers," 1950; New York: Dover Publications, Inc., 1966.

Avery, Madam Susanna. *A Plain Plantain—A Still Room Book.* Originally published in 1688; Falls Village, Connecticut: Herb Growers Press, 1950.

Aylett, Mary. *Herbs in the Garden.* London: Burke, 1955.

Birdseye, Clarence and Eleanor G. *Growing Woodland Plants.* New York: Oxford University Press, 1951; New York: Dover Publications, Inc., 1972.

Blanchan, Neltje. *Wild Flowers Worth Knowing.* New York: Doubleday Page & Co., 1923.

Bland, John. *Forests of Lilliput—The Realm of Mosses and Lichens.* Englewood Cliffs, New Jersey: Prentice Hall, Inc., 1971.

Britton, N. L. and Brown, A. *An Illustrated Flora of the Northern United States and Canada,* 3 volumes. Originally published in 1913 as "An Illustrated Flora of the Northern United States, Canada, and British Possession"; New York: Dover Publications, Inc., 1970.

Brooklyn Botanic Garden. *Dye Plants and Dyeing.* Brooklyn, New York: privately printed, 1970.

Brown, Dr. O. Phelps. *The Complete Herbalist—Nature's Remedies.* Jersey City, New Jersey: privately printed, 1885.

Camp, W. H. "The World in Your Garden," *National Geographic Magazine,* July 1947.

Claire, Colin. *Of Herbs & Spices.* London: Abelard-Schuman, 1961.

Clarkson, Rosetta E. *Green Enchantment.* New York: The Macmillan Co., 1940; Reprinted in 1972 under title "Golden Age of Herbs and Herbalists."

——. *Herbs, Their Culture and Uses.* New York: The Macmillan Co., 1971.

——. *Magic Gardens.* New York: The Macmillan Co., 1939.

Cobb, Boughton. *A Field Guide to Ferns.* Boston: Houghton Mifflin Co., 1956.

Cockayne, Oswold (ed.) *Leechdoms, Wortcunning and Starcraft of Early England.* London: Longmans Green, 1865; Facsimile edition, the British Museum, 1955.

Coles, William. *The Art of Simpling.* Originally published in London, 1657; Facsimile reprint, Rosetta E. Clarkson, Milford, Connecticut, 1938.

Coon, Nelson. *Using Plants for Healing.* New York: Hearthside Press, Inc., 1963.

——. *Using Wayside Plants.* New York: Hearthside Press, Inc., 1960.

Crowhurst, Adrienne. *The Weed Cookbook.* New York: Lancer Books, 1972.

Culpeper, Nicholas. *Culpeper's Complete Herbal.* London: Foulsham & Co., Ltd., New York: distributed by Sterling Publishing Co., Inc.

De-Bairacli-Levy, Juliette. *Herbal Handbook for Everyone.* London: Faber & Faber, 1966.

Evelyn, John. *Acetaria, A Discourse of Sallets.* Originally published in 1699; Facsimile edition, Brooklyn Botanic Garden, 1937.

Fernald, Merritt Lyndon and Kinsey, Alfred Charles. *Edible Wild Plants of Eastern North America*. Originally published by Harvard College, 1943; New York: Harper & Row, 1958.

Fernald, Merritt Lyndon. *Gray's Manual of Botany*, 8th ed. New York: American Book Co., 1950.

Foster, Gertrude B. *Herbs for Every Garden*. New York: E. P. Dutton & Co., Inc., 1966.

Fox, Helen Morganthau. *Gardening with Herbs for Flavor and Fragrance*. New York: The Macmillan Co., 1936.

Freeman, Margaret B. *Herbs for the Mediaeval Household*. New York: Metropolitan Museum of Art, 1943.

Gerard, John. *The Herball or General Historie of Plantes*. Originally published 1597; 2nd edition by Thomas Johnson published in 1636; London: Spring Books, 1927.

Gibbons, Euell. *Stalking the Healthful Herbs*. New York: David McKay Co., Inc., 1970.

———. *Stalking the Wild Asparagus*. New York: David McKay Co., Inc., 1962.

Gordon, Jean. *The Art of Cooking with Roses*. New York: Walker & Co., 1968.

Greenaway, Kate. *Language of Flowers*. New York: Merrimack Publishing Corp.

Grieve, Mrs. Maude. *A Modern Herbal*, 2 volumes. New York: Harcourt, Brace & Co., 1931; New York: Dover Publications, Inc., 1971.

Gunther, Robert T. *The Greek Herbal of Dioscorides*. Originally published as "Byzantine AD 512" and "Englished by Joun Goodyear, 1655"; London: Hafner Publishing Co., 1933; Facsimile editions, 1934 and 1959.

Harding, A. R. *Ginseng and Other Medicinal Plants*. Columbus, Ohio: A. R. Harding Publishing Co., 1908.

Harris, Ben Charles. *Eat the Weeds*. Barre, Massachusetts: Barre Publishers, 1971.

———. *The Compleat Herbal*. Barre, Massachusetts: Barre Publishers, 1972.

Hatfield, Audrey Wynne. *How to Enjoy Your Weeds*. New York: Sterling Publishing Co., Inc., 1971.

Hayes, Elizabeth S. *Spices and Herbs Around the World*. Garden City, New Jersey: Doubleday & Co., 1961.

Hedrick, U. P. *History of Horticulture in America to 1860*. New York: Oxford University Press, 1950.

———. *Sturtevant's Edible Plants of the World*. Originally published as "Sturtevant's Notes on Edible Plants" by J. B. Lyon Co., Albany in 1919 as the Department of Agriculture's 27th Annual Report; New York: Dover Publications, Inc., 1972.

Herbst, Josephine. *New Green World*. New York: Hastings House, 1954.

Hinds, Harold R. and Hathaway, Wilfred A. *Wildflowers of Cape Cod*. Chatham, Massachusetts: The Chatham Press, Inc., 1968.

Hollingsworth, Buckner. *Flower Chronicles*. New Brunswick, New Jersey: Rutgers University Press, 1958.

Houseman, Ethel Henckley. *Beginner's Guide to Wild Flowers*. New York: G. P. Putnam's Sons, 1948.

Hulme, F. Edward, FLS, FSA. *Familiar Wild Flowers*, 5 volumes. London: Cassell & Co. Ltd., (1897?).

Kamm, Minnie Watson. *Old Time Herbs for Northern Gardens*. Boston: Little, Brown & Co., 1938; New York: Dover Publications, Inc., 1971.

Keeler, Harriet L. *Our Garden Flowers*. New York: Charles Scribner's Sons, 1922.

Kerr, Jessica. *Shakespeare's Flowers*. New York: Thomas Y. Crowell Co., 1969.

Kingsbury, John M. *Deadly Harvest*. New York: Holt, Rinehart & Winston, 1965.

Law, Donald. *Herb Growing for Health*. New York: Arco Publishing Co., 1969.

Leighton, Ann. *Early American Gardens "For Meate or Medicine."* Boston: Houghton Mifflin Co., 1970.

Leyel, Mrs. C. F. *Herbal Delights*. London: Faber & Faber Ltd., 1937.

Lindsay, T. S. B. D. Archdeacon of Dublin. *Plant Names*. London, New York & Toronto: Sheldon Press; New York: The Macmillan Co., 1923.

Loewenfeld, Claire. *Herb Gardening*. London: Faber & Faber, Ltd., 1964.

Medsger, Oliver Perry. *Edible Wild Plants*. New York: The Macmillan Co., 1939.

Meyer, Joseph E. *The Herbalist*. Hammond, Indiana: Indiana Botanic Garden, 1972.

Mitchell, Sydney B. *Iris for Every Garden*. New York: M. Barrows & Co., Inc., 1960.

Muenscher, Walter C. and Rice, Myron A. *Garden Spice and Wild Pot Herbs*. Ithaca, New York: Cornell University Press, 1955.

Murphy, Edith Van Allen. *Indian Uses for Native Plants*. Palm Desert, California: Desert Printers, Inc. 1959.

Murray, J. M. and Nicoll, W. *Toilet of Flora—1779*. London: privately printed, 1779; Milford, Connecticut: Rosetta E. Clarkson, 1939.

Northcote, Lady Rosalind. *The Book of Herb Lore*. Originally published in London in 1912 as "Book of Herbs"; New York: Dover Publications, Inc., 1971.

Peterson, Roger Tory and McKenny, Margaret. *A Field Guide to Wild Flowers*. Boston: Houghton Mifflin Co., 1968.

Quelch, Mary Thorne. *Herbs for Daily Use in Home, Medicine and Cookery*. London: Faber & Faber Ltd., 1969.

Ranson, Florence. *British Herbs*. Hammondsworth, Middlesex: Penguin Books Ltd., 1954.

Rohde, Eleanor Sinclair. *Herbs and Herb Gardening*. New York: Macmillan Co., 1937.

———. *The Old English Herbals*. Originally published in 1922; New York: Dover Publications, Inc., 1971.

Sanford, S. N. F. *New England Herbs, Their Preparation and Use*. Boston: New England Museum of Natural History, 1937.

Seymour, Frank Conklin. *The Flora of New England*. Rutland, Vermont: Charles E. Tuttle Co., 1969.

Squires, Mabel. *The Art of Drying Plants & Flowers*. New York: Bonanza Books, 1958.

Syme, John T. Boswell (ed.) *English Botany; or Coloured Figures of British Plants*, 12 volumes, London: Robert Hardwicke, 1863–1872.

Taylor, Raymond L. *Plants of Colonial Days*. Williamsburg, Virginia: Colonial Williamsburg, Inc., 1952.

Thomson, Richard. *Old Roses for Modern Gardens*. Princeton, New Jersey: D. Van Nostrand Co., Inc., 1959.

U.S. Dept. of Agriculture. *American Medicinal Plants of Commercial Importance*. Government Printing Office, 1930.

———. *Common Weeds of the United States*. Government Printing Office, 1970; New York: Dover Publications, Inc., 1971.

———. *Production of Drug and Condiment Plants*. Government Printing Office, 1948.

Verrill, A. Hyatt. *Perfumes and Spices, Including an Account of Soaps & Cosmetics*. Boston: L. C. Page & Co., 1945.

Webster, Helen Noyes. *Herbs, How to Grow Them and How to Use Them*. Newton, Massachusetts: Chas. T. Branford Co., 1959.

Wilder, Louise Beebe. *The Fragrant Path*. New York: The Macmillan Co., 1932.

Williams, Katherine Barnes. *Herbs: The Spice of a Gardener's Life*. Kansas City, Missouri: Diversity Books, 1965.

Woodward, Marcus. *Leaves from Gerard's Herball*. From "The Herball or General Historie of Plantes," originally published 1597. New York: Dover Publications, Inc., 1969.

Yanovsky, Elias. *Food Plants of the North American Indians*. Government Printing Office, 1936.

Index of Common Names

Page numbers in italics refer to illustrations.

Index of Scientific Names

Page numbers in italics refer to illustrations.